My Father's Shadow

My Father's Shadow

a memoir

Sandra Goldbloom Zurbo

MONASH
UNIVERSITY
PUBLISHING

Published by Monash University Publishing
Matheson Library Annexe
40 Exhibition Walk
Monash University
Clayton, Victoria 3800, Australia
publishing.monash.edu

Monash University Publishing: the discussion starts here

 A catalogue record for this book is available from the National Library of Australia

9781922979186 (paperback)
9781922979193 (pdf)
9781922979209 (epub)

Cover design by Les Thomas
Typesetting by Cannon Typesetting
Author photograph by Harry Nankin

Printed in Australia by Griffin Press

Fathers have fantasies how their daughters should be, lovers have fantasies how their brides should be, and if a woman has not a strong feeling of identity she will very much be tempted to play up to the stage and then she becomes what we call an 'anima woman'. She plays the role that men expect from her and loses her own identity. This is a very widespread and very dangerous thing for women[,] which generally leads to disaster.

Marie-Louise von Franz, Reflections on Jungian Psychology,
1975

Remembering is always shot through with fiction …
Siri Hustvedt, What I Loved, *in an interview with Claire Nichols,*
The Book Show, *ABC Radio National, 2019*

By Way of an Introduction

My father, political activist Samuel Mark Goldbloom, was my hero and nemesis all the days of his life. A controversial public figure from the late 1950s, when in 1959 he became the founding secretary of the Congress for International Cooperation and Disarmament (CICD), he remained for the next forty years a significant peace and anti-nuclear activist on the national and international stages. He was also an active member of the Jewish Council to Combat Fascism and Anti-Semitism, founding secretary of the Vietnam Moratorium Campaign, a secret member of the Communist Party of Australia, a Soviet loyalist and a national and international philanderer.

Sam Goldbloom was loved and admired by as many as he was reviled by, particularly – though not only – during the era of the Cold War. Few really knew the truth of this, yet conservatives despised him for his presumed communist affiliation and his Left-wing politics. Many in the Jewish community held him in contempt for his denial of antisemitism in the Soviet Union, a country whose political system he turned an uncritical, even adoring, eye to. The Soviet Union's demise, which came eighteen months before his own, rocked his foundations.

What, after a lifelong defence of, devotion to, the Soviet Union and its allies, had his life, his loyalty, meant?

~

Mystery surrounds many of the stories he told about his life. True, he was a flight mechanic in the airforce during the war. But was he in New Guinea? Did he really learn Japanese to act for the Australian armed forces as an interpreter of Japanese prisoners of war – he who could speak very little Yiddish and barely a word of any other non-English language? What about the story he told of his father pretending to beat him at the behest of his cruel mother? Was that true – or did his father really beat him?

And what of the women? The national and international women? No mystery there.

~

Over the years, as the Middle East conflict grew to be more and more sharply drawn, his support of the Palestine Liberation Organization resulted in many dinner-table arguments between my parents. Criticisms of his position, often venomous, were published in Jewish newspapers and were heard in the community at large; his views on the Middle East sometimes led to disagreements with his friends.

~

Imperialism, colonialism, racism, the glorious Soviet Union, the equally glorious People's Republic of China until, in the early 1960s, the Chinese and Soviet paths, already beginning to diverge, completely split once and for all, at which time the Chinese Party became to him 'those ultra-leftist bastards'. The working class, the capitalist class, wars of independence, the ALP, the DLP ('traitorous bastards') and military spending. May Day, peace marches, antiracism marches and the like were part of many a weekend outing. This is what I was raised on.

~

His impact on me was profound. Politically at least, I was in his thrall, an adoring, loyal and often uncritical daughter. A daughter who, for many years – decades – followed his path into peace activism and defence of the Soviet Union.

Many of my memories are filled with love, remembrance of good times: beach holidays and country picnics. With learning – books, music, film. Some memories are not at all like that. I remember him also with pain, with anger. With rage. But in the end more, much more: with a strong respect and love.

~

Without doubt, having Sam Goldbloom as my father made for an interesting life. Mum, my two sisters and I were warned to be wary of phone taps; I had to learn to become accustomed to being followed to work by … by? … Special Branch? Most likely.

Many national and international peace activists, progressive Labor Party leaders and cultural figures came to dinner at our house. 'Guess who's coming to dinner?' became a catchphrase of our lives. Among the many who dined at our table were Paul and Eslanda

Robeson, Dr Benjamin Spock, Jesse Street, H V Evatt, Linus Pauling, Hollywood actor Danny Kaye and British boogie-woogie pianist Winifred Atwell. Yes, a very interesting life.

~

Some of the stories contained in this book were difficult to write, particularly those I consider, even now, years after he died, to be disloyal to him: the revelation – or confirmation – of secrets, no matter how poorly kept, his brutality towards me, my criticisms of him. Others came more readily, particularly those written in the immediacy of their occurrence, the post-facto moments.

Paradoxically, even though Dad was a public figure, much of his life, particularly his early years, was enigmatic. Questions remain, will always remain. Yet as time passes, continues to pass, my frustration of not knowing – at least not knowing with any certainty – abates.

After all, with no one left to ask, there is no longer any point in it being otherwise.

Number 1

Does he know? I gaze down at him. Does he know he's dying?

He knows alright.

~

Look at him. All rugged up there in his recliner rocker. Snug. Comfortable. He's barely been out of the chair for days. He loves his rocker. When Mum buys it for him, it's brown leather. Over the years, the leather wears out, so they have it re-covered. Now, it's a dusty turquoise colour, though Mum prefers 'aqua', which she pronounces with an Italian accent: *ah-kwah*.

Only his face shows above his lovely. It's a thick mohair blanket that looks like a woolly ocean: all blues and greens and turquoise, soft spikes of mohair rising up like fine ocean spume. Poor circulation means he is often cold, but his lovely keeps him warm as toast. Sister Three and her husband gave it to him. He loves Three.

What a pale face today. As he lay sleeping, I stare. Unabashed. No need for sneaky glances to gauge how he's fairing, to see whether he's awake, or to ponder our past, to consider what I think of him right now, what he thinks of me. A long, hard stare.

Look at him. No guile, no tension, no anxiety. Only peace. What a peaceful peacenik. Sleeping. His breath is soft and even. Is he dreaming of his glory days? Those days when he led thousands, sometimes scores of thousands, through the streets of Melbourne, protesting this or that war? The moratorium campaigns against the Vietnam War? Earlier wars, too, though with fewer demonstrators: Hitler's march on Europe, the war in Korea, invasions of one country by another – usually by the United States of America, the testing of atomic bombs? Antiracism demonstrations? May Day marches?

Or is he dreaming of the women?

∼

It's dinner time in 1950 somethingorother. He arrives home from his first peace conference in Europe, where he meets with the politically like-minded at a World Peace Council conference. Rousing speeches. Tumultuous applause by a community of peace activists. They plan how they will go about saving the world from itself. Save it from US imperialism and the warmongers of all nations. Well, of most nations. The Soviet Union and its ally states, members of the Warsaw Pact, are exempt from their protestations.

At conference end, he visits with a number of peace committees in Western Europe and takes a look around parts of the world where he has never before been.

Mum and Dad, we three sisters and Bubbeh are seated at the dinner table. He talks animatedly, marvels at what he's seen, where he's been taken on his travels; he talks seriously about the meetings he attends. Then, vibrant, excited, he begins to talk about a French journalist he meets at the conference. Despite my age – fourteen – it is clear at once that this is a different kind of animation, and I know it has nothing to do with world peace or the meetings he participates in to strive for it.

He meets Martine at the conference and, after, visits her at home in Paris.

At the dinner table he's talking about her, about the woman in Paris. His new friend. A journalist with the French Communist Party's newspaper, L'Humanité; she is also a novelist and essayist, he says. Smart, he says. 'Martine this …' he says. 'Martine that …'

He has fallen in love. At fourteen, I'm an avid reader of True Romance magazines (at night, by torchlight, under the blankets). I know a thing or two about romance. Yes indeed.

I look at him with new respect. He is so sophisticated, I think. I do not notice – I ignore – Mum, tight-lipped at the other end of the dinner table.

Their affair continues for a good five years, possibly longer, once a year in person when he is in Europe, for the rest by correspondence. When he and the journalist break with each other, their separation is precipitated along Party lines. She becomes an entrenched Maoist, he, until the day the Soviet Union dies, an unerring believer in the Soviet Union. Never again the twain shall meet.

Martine dies in the 1990s. He learns of her death through the international peace movement grapevine. When he tells me, I ask him if he feels sorrowful. At first, his lips tighten, and then he sighs, casts his eyes down. 'Yes,' he says simply. 'I do. I never stopped missing her.'

For all those years, Mum is aware of Martine's existence, just as she is aware of the many others. On one of the rare occasions she accompanies Dad to Europe, the two women meet. Brave wife.

~

I stand beside him. Look at that nose. Dad's shnoz. I smile at it, at him. It's not a Jimmy Durante, but it is the outstanding feature of his long – and, women friends often remark, handsome – face. A large Semitic shnoz.

Mind you, the ears aren't too bad either. Long now, lengthened with age, though they were always long. And quite wide. Big Ears, we sometimes called him when we were kids. He never seemed to mind.

~

His hands are neatly folded on his midriff. Long fingers. Pale, freckled skin. I've always fancied a man with elegant hands, long fingers. It's often the physical feature that first attracts me. Well before the face. Never the body. Hands. Brain. Only rarely the face. Never the body.

I watch him.

Breath in. Breath out. Breath in. Breath out.

A little snore.

Breath in. Breath …

His hair is silvery white. What hair is left. Not that he's ever had much. Not for decades, anyway.

~

The family is seated around the table. A roasted chicken on a platter is surrounded by golden baked potatoes and pumpkin. A bowl of steaming peas, the scent of mint wafting off them, sits alongside. Must be Sunday.

'I used to have more hair, you know,' he says. 'Like this.'

He sweeps his hand over the top of his bald head to describe a Veronica Lake coif of long straight hair that flops over one eye.

'Dad,' we groan, 'not again.' Even Sister Two, who forgives him almost anything.

'Ah ha,' he says, 'you liked it better this way?'

Uses his fingers – those long, elegant fingers – to describe curls. He could just as easily have been making spiders' legs dangling above his head. Milking the joke.

～

Dad's rocker stands beside a teak buffet, along the top of which stand many of the tchatchkes – ornaments, knickknacks – he brings home from his annual travels. My favourite among them is a cream-coloured plastic whirling Dervish whose skirt is fixed in a twirl; his jacket is slightly agape. On his head is a dark red fez. Despite the rigidity of the plastic, everything about the Dervish except his feet gives the impression of movement. After Mum dies and we siblings divvy up the spoils, I claim the Sufi for my own and give him pride of place on top of a low-rise bookcase.

Two months after I bring him home, I accidentally break off one of his brittle plastic feet. Dismayed, I try to glue the foot back on, but I cannot make the parts stick. My little Sufi is hobbled. Now he stands on the bookcase, lopsided. So he exasperatingly remains until I decide there's nothing for it but to try to snap off the other foot and hope that in the course of this amputation I will not break any other body part or rend his clothing. I hope there will be symmetry to the surgery.

I hold my breath. *Snap* go the secateurs.

The surgery works a treat.

～

In one of our conversations, a jazz pianist I befriend tells me he is a Sufi Muslim.

One day, the musician comes to my house. I show him my footless Sufi, which he admires. Later in the year, when he and his family are preparing to move to another state, I offer him the statue, diminished though it is, as my housewarming gift. Happily, my friend accepts the gift and later writes from his new home to tell me that his whirling Dervish has a place of honour there. I am touched.

Next to the Dervish stands a wedding photo. In it, Dad looks the spitting image of the Hollywood actor Basil Rathbone. Dapper, Dad looks, in his air force uniform. And it's true: he does have hair then, thick and wavy and dark. Dark red, he used to say. As well, he sports a pencil-thin moustache. Tall, he is, and thin. Mum says that her mother – our Bubbeh – called him the *lange loksh*. That's Yiddish for long, thin noodle.

'Rayzl,' she'd call from the front door, 'the *lange loksh* has come to see you.' Then she'd burst into unbridled laughter. Every time, though Mum never did understand what was so funny and Bubbeh wasn't telling.

Slowly, quietly, he wakes up. Stretches his arms. Gives a moan of pleasure when he sees me. Smiles.

'Hello, Number 1,' he says, his voice just above a whisper.

His use of this expression makes me smile. Calling me 'Number 1' starts like this.

As I do each day, I phone to see how he's doing.

'Hello, Dad. How are you feeling today?'

'Which one is that?'

'Number 1,' I reply.

He chuckles. 'Hello, Number 1. How are you?'

A lightning bolt of exhilaration shoots through me. The ambiguity of it: my place in the siblings' birth chronology, true enough. But in his heart too?

During the pleasantries we exchange I hear him smile and wonder if he hears me smiling.

~

Now, fully awake, he puts out his hand. I hold it. His skin is dry, warm. 'Hello, Dad. Cup of tea?'

'Thank you, Number 1. That would be lovely.'

And so it goes until he dies. Number 1 he calls me, not always but often, and with a smile. As if we share a secret. Which we do. It's poorly concealed, this secret, but everyone knows.

Number 1, that's me.

On Being Jewish

It is my erroneous belief that Dad isn't at all interested in being Jewish, and so, being an adoring daughter, I shun Jewish myself, pretty much entirely. But around the time I turn fifty, when I begin to think seriously about who his friends have been and are, about how he conducts himself in the world and the organisations he engages with, I realise that I have been mistaken. Being a traditional, not religious, don't believe in god Reform Jew, that is who he has been all his life.

Being Jewish has always been very important to him, I realise. And now, in my fifties, it becomes important to me. I start to go to synagogue and to light the candles on Friday night, the Sabbath, and, thanks to Nico the baker at Babka in Brunswick Street in Fitzroy, cut slices of the small, single person's challah he makes especially for me. Once my grandchildren are old enough to stay overnight, I pass on to them those of the Sabbath rituals and prayers I know. We bless the candles, the bread, the fruit of the vine (which for us is grape juice). We bless the children.

Baruch atta Adonai …

In those early days of return, I cry a lot. My sense of loss, of having dispensed with the richness that is Judaism, is profound.

As well as attending synagogue each week, I join the choir and sing during the High Holy days: Rosh Hashanah, Kol Nidre, Yom Kippur.

Oseh shalom bimromav

Hu ya'aseh shalom aleynu …

~

'Dad,' I say into the phone, 'would you like to come over to talk to me about what being Jewish means to you? I'll make you lunch.'

'That would be lovely, Sandy,' he replies. The eagerness in his voice is unmistakeable.

After we establish a mutually suitable date, we chat for a minute or two longer, say goodbye and then hang up.

Dad is always glad to eat at my house (though there was one occasion when he proclaimed the asparagus to be too undercooked for his liking), so not only will he enjoy my cooking, but he will also have an opportunity to talk about himself with little to no restraint.

Which he does. But, as it transpires, not as I hoped.

~

We buss each other on the cheeks – left, right, left. It's a little performance he enjoys, but one in which I sometimes stumble because I'm never sure if he's going to do the two buss or the three, or on which cheek he's going to start. Then he leads me down my hallway to the large open space at the back of my house: a sunny lounge and dining area, and a long galley-style kitchen that runs the length of the east wall. The other walls are floor to ceiling glass – windows, doors – with views to the back and side gardens, which I have turned from scrappy

Merri Creek clay and weeds into fecund spaces with plants that grow in rich soil, replete with worms as fat as a pinky finger.

Even though Dad has become slightly bent and now needs a walking stick to get around, there is a spring in his step today. He raises a hand to show me he's carrying a small cassette recorder, which he waggles from side to side as he holds up in the air. 'Brought this,' he says. 'Might be good to record our conversation.'

My heart sinks. In that moment I realise this is not going to be an intimate conversation between a father and his daughter; rather, this is to be an interview. He – we – will record his attitudes towards being Jewish for … for what? Whom? Posterity? The University of Melbourne Archive, where some of his documents already reside? Most likely he is unaware of my long, drawn-out sigh.

'What's on for lunch today? Something good, I expect.'

I give him a mock withering look and we burst out laughing. He places the recorder on the dining table, turns and gives me a big hug.

'How are you doing today, Dad?'

What follows is a synopsis of this and that failing body part and where the cancer is up to now. When his recitation is finished, he makes a guttural *akh* sound that rises from the back of his throat. Then, as if what he has just said has become tangible, he waves it all away.

~

Over our meal, we chat about mostly inconsequential matters, a bit of family gossip, a little about politics. Clearly, given the speed with which he downs his food, he's keen to get into an armchair and begin the real conversation.

I make tea and bring the pot and cups to a side table between the armchair where he now sits, and the couch, where I will sit. He plonks the cassette player on the table and asks me to wait a moment while he makes sure it's working properly. (Hope it isn't, I say to myself.) 'Testing, one, two, three …' He plays it back and we hear his voice coming at us out of the recorder's tinny speaker. While he fiddles, I pour the tea and place a couple of sweet biscuits on a plate for him.

'OK,' he says, satisfied. 'Let's begin.'

He is curious about why I want to have this conversation. So I kick things off by telling him that in an illuminating moment I realised that although he was never interested in going to the synagogue unless he had to – births, deaths, marriages, bat or bar mitzvahs – being Jewish is, has always been, important to him. That despite their very wide acquaintance, all my parents' friends, with the exception of Dawn and Vern, are Jewish.

His eyes widen. 'But of course,' he says, shocked. 'It's always been important.' Neither of us has a mobile phone or any other form of camera, so his shock is not – cannot be – captured. I will be the only person to ever see the expression on his face, to hear the astonishment in his voice. There is no visual imprint to demonstrate how surprised he is.

Dad is also surprised when I tell him, shyly, that I have been going to shul every Friday night for most of the past two years. Even more so that for two successive years I sing in the synagogue choir on Kol Nidre and the next day during Yom Kippur. 'You did?' he says, as he raises an eyebrow a scant degree short of astonishment. He pauses to ponder for a minute or two. Neither of us speak; the cassette records the silence. Then: 'Is it satisfying to go? To sing? Do you enjoy it?'

Now it is my turn to be surprised. This is not the sort of question I would ever expect from him.

'I feel as if I've found my way home,' I say. Sitting alone at the back of the room, I tell him, my profound sense of loss is compounded by the melancholy of the prayers sung by the choir and the congregation, led by the kantor and the rabbi. In time, having memorised the words through repetition, I am able to sing the prayers without the need to follow the transliterations at the back of the prayer book.

After, when I tell him – confess? – that I kiss the Torah scroll borne by the rabbi through the synagogue when it passes the pew where I sit, I wait for his explosion, his scepticism.

Neither is forthcoming.

Once again a comfortable silence rests between us. I wait. Then, after another minute or two, I say, 'What are you thinking?' (which probably means 'What do you think?'). He tells me, 'Nothing.' He's not thinking anything, he says.

Liar.

Yet I don't press him. Another few minutes pass, after which he asks me if I believe in God. No, I tell him, smiling, I do not. He seems relieved, though I can't be sure.

It feels as if something more might be elicited from him, something deeper, more personal, a story previously untold perhaps, but I don't know – have never known – how to break through his reticence. Like so many men his age, he keeps much of his life, his past, much of who he wanted to be, who he was and is, to himself. What he does tell, which isn't much, is often recounted in a jocular fashion. Long after he dies, it occurs to me that jocularity is a mode used by Holocaust Jews: survivors, men in particular, to hide their anguish, to protect themselves from their ghastly and ghostly memories.

Our history tells me to be wary, to not to ask any more than he's prepared to give.

Then, the moment passes. And so he begins to interview himself.

∼

Already, after the first five or so minutes, I am bored. How often have I heard these stories? They resemble a historical recounting, as if from the pages of a book. They tell me nothing much about him. Certainly nothing more than I already know. If he thinks I'm getting too close, digging too deep, asking too personal a question – a question that might reveal too much of himself or might contradict his point of view – he brushes me away. Pesky mosquito, me. More than two hours pass.

∼

Only one event he recounts is new to me. In the early 1990s, Dad applies for his Special Branch files. The papers take some time to come, longer than anticipated. When they do, there is not one clean page among the folders. Each is heavily redacted with thick black marker; what remains is as good as useless.

The redactions he shows me detail, we presume, meetings and the comings and goings of leftists, activists, communists and fellow travellers. Little of substance can be gleaned from what remains. Only one item is clear, and what he learns from it shocks him. 'They've left enough material,' he says as he shows me the appropriate pages, 'to make me realise there had been a snitch in the Jewish Council. Someone who was ratting on us to Special Branch.' He is referring to the Jewish Council to Combat Fascism and Anti-Semitism.

Among the many pages of his thick files it is revealed that a member of the Council was a plant, a snitch, a dobber. A rat. One of the people in the organisation, someone he considered to be a fellow Jew, a comrade, a close friend, was not. Whoever this person was, they passed on to Special Branch information about the doings of the Council and its members.

Surely not one among his friends, all of whom are now dead? Someone else – dead or alive – perhaps?

When he tells me about the rat, he looks bewildered, hurt. 'Who could it have been, Sandy?'

Worst of all about having such knowledge is that it chips away at trust. It is soul destroying. Once learnt, it can never be erased from one's mind. Everyone in the group, on the committee, in the branch, at the pub ('You know So and So is a narc, don't you?') becomes suspect. Could it be …? Maybe So and So …?

He has, he continues, wondered and wondered who it might have been, but cannot work it out. During one such meandering, he decides that Person A is the one. In another, a different comrade, Person B. Such is his idealism it depresses him to learn that a fellow Council member – a Jew – has betrayed the organisation and its members.

⌣

Time and conversation pass.

The small tape, now full on both sides, is removed from the player and placed in his shirt pocket. Soon after, he prepares to leave. 'Seen my stick, Sandy?' I retrieve it from where I put it.

'I have a feeling that I didn't give you what you wanted,' he says as we walk single file up the hall, he in front again.

Without doubt he has no idea of the enormity – or the ambiguity – of his statement.

'No, Dad, you didn't.'

By now we are at the front door. He leans his walking stick against the wall, clutches the cassette player and drapes both his arms around me, tight. When he finishes with hugging, he reclaims his stick and shuffles out the door to his car. As is often the case, I am left wanting.

Sister Rae

About three days after we play the game of 'What does it mean to you to be Jewish?', he calls me.

Disconcerted still, he reiterates his bewilderment about the conversation – I'll call it a conversation – being unsatisfactory for me. This time I tell him why: the lack of intimacy and the lack of depth in what he had to say, his reluctance to confide any personal information, the repetition of stories I've heard so many times.

After the short silence that follows, he changes gear. His voice begins to vibrate with excitement. 'Well, I'm sorry you feel like that, Sandra, but something good did come out of it, for me at least.'

Our meeting puts him in mind of his sister, Rae, who he has not seen or spoken with for at least fifty years. As he anticipates, it is easy enough, with assistance from the Jewish community grapevine, to find her. Rae has been living in the same apartment in Bondi for decades, he learns, possibly for as long as it has been since they last saw each other. 'I've booked a flight,' he says. 'I'm going up to see her. Leaving on Thursday.'

There's no point expressing concern about his health, about his energy levels and other clucky mother hen worries. He would just brush me aside; besides, he has Mum for that. Instead, I tell him how happy I am for him (which I am). We chat a while longer; then we hang up.

⌒

A little background.

Dad is the second son of Alexander Goldbloom, a Russian Jewish Anglophile who, when he moves from Europe to Australia, irons the accent out of his English and sports tweed coats, stitched leather gloves and homburg hats, and Frances Hart, a stylish, snobbish British Jew, whose British family has been traced back to 1066. Frances is Alexander's second wife, a fact quite possibly unknown to her at the time of their marriage. Before Alexander marries Frances, he and his two brothers live for some years in Australia, where Alexander marries his first wife, Rachel. Around 1911 Rachel dies giving birth to their daughter, Rae. When Rae is about two years old, Alexander leaves her in Melbourne in the care of one of his brothers and this brother's wife and sets sail for England.

Two or three years pass. In a letter to his brother, Alexander writes to say he is stuck in England because of the war. *Please look after my daughter until my return.* While waiting to get back to Australia, he meets, courts and marries Frances; they have two sons, Braham and Samuel Mark.

Eventually, in 1922, when Samuel is two and a half, possibly three, Alexander brings his new family to Australia. Frances does not take to the girl child Rae; she is mean and unloving towards her. Although Rae sometimes stays with them, for the most part she continues to live with her uncle and his wife. Around the time of her late teens, Rae disappears from Dad's life; he rarely sees her again.

17

Alexander holds on long enough to see his son Samuel through his bar mitzvah. A year later, at the age of fifty-four, he dies of a heart attack. A year after Alexander dies, Samuel, now aged fourteen, leaves home. He hits the road and spends the next several years finding work wherever he can and living in boarding houses. Years later, his brother Braham dies, also at the age of fifty-four. Much later still, some time after that fateful birthday, Dad will say that the year he turned fifty-four was the most anxious year of his life.

~

Regarding Rae, Frances never relents. I have come to believe that, until she arrives in Australia, or at least until some time after they board ship for Australia, Frances is never told about Alexander's first marriage, and certainly not about the child Rae.

This belief can only ever be conjecture because there's no one left to ask. When I ask Mum, she shrugs and says, 'Don't know. No idea.' It is clear she also has no interest. There is no love lost between Mum and her mother-in-law.

For me, this is a possible explanation of Frances' eternal hostility towards Rae.

~

Over the years, every now and then Dad hears snippets of news about his sister. He has no idea whether she hears anything about him, although, given his public identity as an activist – newspaper articles, radio and television interviews, vilification in some of the Jewish newspapers regarding his denial of Soviet antisemitism and his support of PLO leader Yasser Arafat – it's likely that she learns much. Still, neither makes contact.

Now, through the Jewish grapevine, it takes him only three days to find her. She sounds as delighted to hear from him, he says, as he is to have found her. At the end of the week he will take a plane to Sydney.

Up, up and away.

~

On his return, he calls. They talked for hours, he tells me. When he becomes tired, he naps. As soon as he wakes, she makes tea and they talk some more. And more still, into the night.

'The one thing I can't understand, Sandy,' he says, 'is that she is still angry with our father for abandoning her. After all this time.' I imagine he is shaking his head.

I sigh, loudly. 'Oh, Dad,' I say, 'of course she is.'

'But why? It's been such a long time.'

'Because you never completely get over something like that.'

'Like what?'

'Like being abandoned.'

We sit together, each comfortably silent on our respective ends of the phone. Then, a little more subdued, he says, 'Well, it was thrilling to see her. We couldn't stop talking.' Another pause, as if he's uncertain whether to add more. He makes up his mind. 'I'm going back soon.'

~

Several trips are made to visit Rae. Each time is an enormous pleasure for both of them. After a year or so of visits, Rae invites him to come to Sydney for the party she's giving for her eightieth birthday. A few friends will be there …

Rae also invites her sister-in-law, but Mum declines. She uses her fear of flying to beg off, but she and Dad could have driven together, or gone by train. No, it is clear that she is somehow threatened by, possibly jealous of, this renewed family connection her husband has made, though the reason never becomes apparent. Indeed, it is never spoken of.

It is also possible that Dad does not encourage Mum to come with him so he can have his sister to himself, without his formally polite, distant with strangers wife at his side.

~

When Dad arrives at Rae's apartment on the weekend of her birthday party, he is exhausted. 'I'm just going to have a little lie down,' he says. Rae tells him what time the visitors are expected. In the now familiar guest room, he lays his head on the pillow and falls into a sound sleep.

When he wakes, it is early evening. He scrubs up, combs his hair, approaches the leadlight double doors that open from the hallway into the lounge room and walks through. Rae is there with her guests – family and friends. She walks over to Dad, links her arm through his and says, 'Dear family and friends, this is my long lost brother, Shmuel.' According to Dad's telling, everyone in the room quietly applauds and steps forward to shake his hand. He was overwhelmed, he says, and couldn't help crying. Just a bit.

~

Not long after, just a few months, Rae phones to say she has breast cancer. She will have the treatments but the doctors aren't very hopeful. Nor is Rae. Dad books the earliest possible flight and hastens to Sydney.

Rae is right to be pessimistic. Her decline is so rapid that in less than a year she is dead. Her brother is heartbroken.

A week or so after he returns home from Rae's funeral, we go for coffee. He repeats what he said to me, by now, two years earlier. 'I know that conversation we had bothered you, and that's your end of it, but I will always be grateful to you because it put Rae into my mind again. The time we had together was ...' The sentence hangs in the air, but there is no need to complete it. I know how much it meant to him.

He looks down at the table, then up at me as if he is about to say something, but once again he can't decide whether to.

'What?' I say. He looks a little embarrassed. 'Tell me.'

'Mmm.' He clears his throat. 'Alright.' He moves around a little on his chair, then: 'Each time I visited Rae, I ... ah ... I did the customary thing with the mezuzah.' He coughs again, then glares at me as if daring me to criticise him.

'You touched the mezuzah and kissed your fingers?'

'Keep your voice down,' he says. Then, 'Yes. It just seemed the right thing to do, to do that, there.'

There it is. Being Jewish is important to him because he is Jewish. He is Jewish because that is how he was born and raised, that is the world to which he belongs. He is not religious and – after he completes his bar mitzvah – will never be. Yet he is a man of faith. His faith lies not in the synagogue or the texts of the holy book but elsewhere, and although it has the same fervour as an intense pious belief, his piety is secular. He calls it communism.

21

~

Even though I continue to feel dissatisfied with what Dad taped (Whatever happened to that tape? Since his death, I have never been able to find it anywhere), I do understand about Dad's relationship to Judaism. Through our conversation, I come to fully appreciate what Judaism means to me and my reclamation of it. To come into the light is to realise there is a place to belong.

~

Light years ago – or so it seems – I sticky tape a Leunig cartoon to the inside of my front door. The cartoon depicts a man sitting up in his bed; his wife stands at the window, looking out. Forlorn, his head slumped, the man says, 'I want to go home.' Puzzled, the wife points out familiar objects in their bedroom to reassure him: 'Here's this ... there's that ... You are at home.' But the man, not at all reassured, continues with his plaint. The woman continues to point out objects in the room, items they can see from the bedroom window, trying to convince her husband that he's just where he wants to be, home. In the cartoon's last frame, the man sits slumped in his bed, dejected; his wife stands at the window. The man says, 'I want to go home.'

The cartoon man's longing – the desire to belong – is, at the time of my reading of this cartoon, instantly recognisable. That man is me.

~

In the end, Dad's reasons and my reasons are the same. He is – we are – Jewish because we are Jewish. It's as simple as that.

22

Crimes, Punishments
and a Bit of Screaming

There are times, most often in my younger years and teens, when I hate him. He wallops me severely for the crimes I commit: stealing cigarettes from his or Mum's cartons, smoking cigarettes, wagging school, going out somewhere I've been banned from going (the wilds of Fitzroy Street, for example), sneaking in through my bedroom window past my humiliatingly early curfew, particularly after being sprung when I sneak out through my bedroom window to meet up with a boy parked down the Alma Road hill who is waiting to take me back to Reata so I can continue listening to folk music. Answering back, however, heads the list.

Answer back? Expect a whack.

One punishment he threatens – but never carries out – is to send me away to boarding school. Send me, *please* send me, I beseech, silently, never out loud. I imagine a *Girls' Own* life of secret adventures and midnight feasts, of staunch unbreakable friendships. When he presents me with another political harangue, I offer my silent contempt. If my answer to a political question is incorrect or I don't agree with his view, he repays me with humiliation: 'Don't be stupid, Sandra' (Stupid, stupid, stupid, he says). Although he doesn't say it as a punishment, not consciously anyway, I wince when he says 'G'day Fatty.' And more.

~

With some of my pocket money I buy a Staedtler HB lead pencil. In its appearance and use, this pencil, with its black and red stripes, its lead that glides across the paper, is an object of beauty. I love this pencil. Copperplates, too, but not as much as the Staedtlers.

When I show him, I am glowing with pleasure. 'Look what I bought, Dad. Isn't it beautiful?'

'This pencil is made in Germany,' he says as he peers at the gold text impressed into one of the black stripes.

Oh no; I recognise that tone. Trouble's coming.

'You know we don't buy German goods in this house,' he says in his stern voice. 'How many times do I have to tell you?' He is referring to the postwar boycott of German goods practised by Jews around the world. In our household this boycott is adhered to as an act of solidarity, as strictly as if we ourselves have been touched by the Holocaust, even though we have not.

'But Dad …'

'Go to your room.' He sighs his what am I going to do with you sigh.

Every part of my body is scrunched up, knotted, as I await the consequences of my misdemeanour. A walloping is on its way. Yeow.

~

One evening a few years after Dad dies, Mum insists on driving me home after dinner at her house. In the milder weather I walk, take a bus, flag down a taxi. Tonight, I accept her offer and off we go. As we now do regularly, we sit in her car out the front of my apartment building opposite Peanut Farm in St Kilda, talking. Tonight the conversation falters before it turns to Dad.

Gazing out the windscreen, she says, 'He used to cry himself to sleep because of what he did to you, you know.'

Inside the car, the air becomes heavy, even though the door on the passenger side is open and there is a sea breeze. My heart is racing. Several minutes pass – it feels like several – before I am able to speak. Finally, my voice strained, low, croaky, I say: 'Well, he never said anything to me. He never apologised.'

Mum is silent. Her gaze remains on the windscreen.

Into the silence slithers a thought. 'Did he ever wallop Sister Two?' Sister Three is never walloped. Instinctively, I am so certain of this that I don't bother to ask. Some time ago I asked Two if she had any recollection of being walloped by Dad. She didn't think so, she said, which was answer enough.

Mum turns in her seat to face me. 'You don't think I was going to let him have both of you, do you?'

Her look – what is it: scorn? incredulity? – chills me.

Rendered speechless, I sit in the silence for a moment, immobilised, and then, coldly, I thank her for the lift, bid her goodnight (no kiss) and get out of the car. Inside the apartment, I drop down on my bed, bury my face in a pillow and scream. I scream and I scream and I scream.

～

As the years pass, as the therapy kicks in, as the hurts and humiliations diminish and fade to grey, the emotional pain of their execution also diminishes, though never entirely. They are never completely forgotten, never completely forgiven. Once I begin to see the world through a psychological lens, I come to believe the unexpressed resentments, frustrations and angers he feels towards Mum (and, most likely, towards his own mother) are frequently meted out to me, and that often in enduring his punishments I am her – their – surrogate.

He loves me, he loves me not. His is loving/brutal, generous/ punitive, fun/demeaning. Mixed messages. These messages will confound me all of my life.

Now You Are a Woman

Something sticky is happening between my legs. Oh no, have I wet myself? How could that be? No, no, I have not. Oh no, can this be my period? It's my period, I'm sure of it. What will I do? I've never had one before. Oh no, everyone will see, everyone will know. Mum's not here. She wins a raffle, an ocean-liner trip to Israel, so she and a friend take off. We sisters are left with Dad to look after us. Who cooks? He can't boil water without burning it. Who cleans? The best he ever musters is removing a plate or two from the dinner table, an occasional run over the living-room floor with the carpet sweeper. Who makes the beds? Never in his life, except, most likely, when he is in the airforce has he made a bed. Must be Bubbeh, who by now has been living with us for about seven years. Yet, in my mind's eye, Bubbeh is not present.

I raise my hand to ask the teacher for permission to go to the toilet. An hour seems to pass before she turns to acknowledge me.

'Yes, Sandra?'

'Miss, may I please leave the room?' Such is the 1950s euphemism when a student asks permission to go to the toilet.

'Very well, Sandra,' she says, 'but no smoking.'

How does she know that, at thirteen, I smoke cigarettes? My curiosity is fleeting, my fear that I might have bled through my unders urgent.

In the toilet, my worst fear is realised: there is blood in the crutch of my white panties. Oh no. What am I going to do? Who can I tell? I don't have any pads. Racked with mortification, gulping down tears, I succumb: there's only one thing for it.

～

At the headmaster's office, the school secretary looks up when I come through the door.

'Hello, Sandra,' she says, smiling. 'In trouble again?' She continues to smile.

'No,' I say, feeling the burn on my cheeks. 'No, I ... um ... I ...'

Before I am able to blurt out my sentence, the secretary stands up from her desk, strides around to where I stand and puts her hand on my shoulder. 'Did you get your period?'

Oh no, she said it out loud. I glance towards the headmaster's closed office door. Is he in there, listening?

The secretary smiles again and pats me on the arm. 'It's alright,' she says. 'Happens to all of us females. Hmm, your mother's away, isn't she?' I nod. 'Very well, come with me.'

We go together to the sick room. There is a bed in there, a table and a chair, a cupboard as well where classroom and office supplies are kept – chalk, blackboard dusters, reams of paper, pencils, boxes of brass drawing pins, typewriter ribbons. Menstrual pads and belts. When she opens the cupboard door, I see a gleaming white first-aid box with a red cross painted on its front. She removes some items from the cupboard, turns back to me and hands me a face washer. 'I'm going to leave you in here to wash yourself. When you've finished, wrap the washer in this newspaper and leave it in the bin under the sink. After that, you'll need these.' She holds open a brown paper bag. Peering inside, I see a Modess menstrual pad and an elastic belt with two metal clips attached to it. It's designed to hold the pad firmly in place, to ensure that it doesn't slip around in or fall out of the wearer's knickers. 'Do you know what to do with them? Did your mother show you?'

Why won't the floor open up, swallow me whole? 'Well … yes, sort of.'

The secretary explains how I should attach the pad to the belt's loops, then step into each of the two created spaces – 'Yes, through there' – and pull up the contraption until I feel comfortable. She suggests I not worry too much about the blood in my panties. 'It's almost time for the bell, so you can leave school now and wash them when you get home.' As she exits the room, she turns and says, 'Come to see me when you're ready.'

'What about my class? Mrs Teacher will wonder where I am.'

'Don't you worry about that. I'll take care of it.'

Before I leave school, the secretary gives me a supply of four pads. 'When you get home, tell you father. He'll look after you.'

When I get home I remove the bloodied underpants, wrap them and the pad in several sheets of newspaper and secrete the parcel under the rubbish already in the bin. Tonight is rubbish night, which means tomorrow morning the garbo will come and take away the evidence.

⁓

29

Although I see only a little blood, I change pads often. As a result my supply runs out by morning. Now I'm going to have to tell him. I go to his bedroom and stand in the doorway.

'Good morning, Dad,' I say, timid. 'I …'

'Good morning, Sandy. What's up?'

'I got my period.'

At once he smiles, sits up straight, moves to the centre of the bed and pats the space he's vacated, inviting me to sit there. When I sit, twisting to face him, he places a hand on each side of my face, dips my head and places a gentle kiss on my forehead. Then, in keeping with Jewish tradition, but without the severity of the traditional slap – the metaphor for life's harshness that awaits a woman from the onset of menstruation – he pats me once on my cheek and says, in keeping with custom, 'Now you are a woman. Mazel tov. Good onya, Sandy,' and gives me a hug.

Which leads to a round of bawling.

'There, there,' he says. He takes a hankie from under his pillow and passes it to me. 'Here, blooz. You mother said this might happen while she is away. She left supplies for you.'

He gets out of bed and goes to the wardrobe. 'Here,' he says as he dangles a string bag in front of me, 'a couple of packets of pads and two or three belts.'

My face is beetroot red, I can tell. My cheeks, my neck, my whole face – on fire.

'Are you OK?' Closely, he watches my face.

'Yes.'

'Alright, then. Off you go. Get ready for school. Tonight we'll have a celebration.'

He hugs me again, and then releases me.

~

For many periods to come, I wriggle in my desk during class in the hope that I am not leaking blood that will stain my school uniform, enabling everyone to see … what? It doesn't occur to me that most, if not all, the other girls are bleeding too.

In the toilet block at recess and at lunchtime, I check my uniform for bloodstains. There are none, but that doesn't stop me from worrying. I carry this anxiety with me for the remainder of my teenage school years. Four.

~

What I don't tell the secretary, what I don't tell Dad or Mum or anyone, ever, is that the bloody leakage – which feels more like a torrent, like a haemorrhage – smells sweet to me, like honey.

Everything Turns to Ash

After Gorbachev had long gone, the old apparatchiks had become the new Mafia and the Mafia had taken over, all the hopes and aspirations that [he] felt deeply became a chimera; they were gone.

The author, quoting her father, in an interview with
Michael Hamel-Green, 2022

A Radio National guest discusses the book he's written about the 1956 Soviet invasion of Hungary. After a while my ears prick up.

Until that day, the day of the RN program, I believe – as Dad believes – this upsurge is not a popular uprising of the people but one instigated by the CIA. Many communists and fellow travellers support the CIA theory. Many do not; so disgusted are these members by this aggression they leave the Party. After the purges, the antisemitism, the authoritarianism, the invasion is, for them, the final straw.

At first I pay scant attention to the author and his interviewer; their voices are mere background murmur, white noise. After a while, though, the words 'Hungary', 'Soviet tanks' and '1956' worm their way into my consciousness and I begin to heed what is being said.

Which leads me to wonder. What if the CIA plot story isn't true? What if it is a Party line? A line promulgated by Party members and fellow travellers who, at that time and for the most part, are as devout supporters of the Soviet Union as is Dad? This is a possibility I have never contemplated.

The author's voice is mellow. He is persuasive, lucid, calm. It is this absence of vitriol, the lack of intense emotion, high dudgeon, that catches my attention. I suppose it's plausible that, given the amount of time that's passed between the event and the day I'm listening to the radio – fifty years – what was once the rage of the broadcaster's guest has diminished. Perhaps he is a historian who has never had any emotional investment in this story.

What if this quietly spoken academic is saying something that's true? If it is, what might it mean about what I believe? About how blindly I followed Dad's views?

Many years after the event, decades after, I come to believe that, somewhere in the middle of the two stories about the 1956 events in Hungary – a grassroots people's uprising and a full-on CIA intervention – lies the truth.

～

Before he dies our views begin to differ. Even more so today, twenty years after he dies, my views would differ from his and lead to arguments between us. In time, some years before Dad dies, what I begin to see more clearly – my blind political adherence, my obedience – is too humiliating to contemplate.

33

Slightly, a heavy door creaks open. For the time being, I slam the door shut. Hard.

~

As for Dad, when it comes to the Union of Soviet Socialist Republics – the USSR – and its satellites, he is a fool for love. He will truck no criticism about any of the socialist states: he does not acknowledge the purges or the millions murdered, he will never acknowledge the antisemitism, though later, much later, he will describe Gorbachev's perestroika and glasnost as 'a breath of fresh air'. Still, for most of his life, Dad's belief in the Soviet Union, in its form of socialism, remains devout in scope. With the demise of communism – first with the bricks and mortar of the Berlin Wall, subsequently in the other nations of the Warsaw Pact and finally in the Soviet Union – his heart breaks.

Here is a domino theory he could never – *would* never – have envisaged.

He says little else about what that demise means to him, what it means about a lifetime of loyalty and belief demolished.

Even so, he will remain a socialist for the years of his life left to him, despite the fact that, as I once heard someone say – Tariq Ali, perhaps – the Soviets gave socialism such a bad name.

Sandra and Sammy
Go to the Movies

Mum is in Fairfield Infectious Diseases Hospital. She's been there for weeks being pricked and prodded while doctors attempt to ascertain what it is that's laid her low. When the doctors say to her, 'We don't yet know what it is you've got, Mrs Goldbloom, but don't worry, it's not terminal', she is not reassured.

'If you don't know what it is,' she snips at them, 'how do you know it isn't terminal?'

Mum reports that they smile at her – condescendingly, she believes – and leave the ward. When she tells this story, I imagine white-coated doctors patting her on the head.

After three months or so, still without a diagnosis, Mum is discharged from the hospital. It will be years – not until the mid to late 1960s – before her diagnosis is given a name: polymyalgia rheumatica.

~

In the year of Mum's hospitalisation, the 1959 Melbourne Film Festival begins without her. She and Dad have tickets to several screenings, as they have every year since the festival's inception.

With Mum unable to go, Dad asks if I would like to attend with him on her ticket.

You bet.

Already I love film. From the time I am very young, younger than ten, Bubbeh takes me to her favourites, American musicals, often more than once: *Seven Brides for Seven Brothers*, *Oklahoma*, *The Great Caruso*, *The Eddie Cantor Story*, *Brigadoon*, *Guys and Dolls*, *Kismet* … You get the idea. By the time Dad invites me to join him at the film festival I am already old enough to go regularly with friends to Saturday afternoon matinees, later, to Friday or Saturday night pictures at one of the many cinemas in and around St Kilda – the Palais, the Victory, the Astor and the two Metros.

Planning the year's film festival selections becomes one of the most thrilling events in my teenage life, even after the advent of rock'n'roll. Everything about film thrills me: sitting in the dark watching, listening, thinking. How luxurious. How delectable. My love for film never wanes, even when, many years later, most of my watching is done on a screen in my lounge room.

～

Dressed up neat casual, we're ready to go.

In the foyer of the Rivoli we greet family friends, quite a few of them Eastern and central European Jews, Holocaust escapees and survivors, as well as people we know more casually, including political colleagues, most of them Dad's age. In Robert Menzies' 1950s button-down Australia, while grateful for the haven Australia offers them, these people hunger for a level of culture they have had to leave behind in Poland, Czechoslovakia, Germany, Austria. In time that will come, but for a while yet, outside of their own social and cultural communities, what they have is the film festival, a Melbourne Symphony Orchestra concert that sometimes includes a visiting soloist, a cafe or restaurant, a community event – and being called 'wog', 'Yid', 'refo'.

The air is thick with conversation, laughter and cigarette smoke. At the snack shop patrons line up to buy popcorn, lollies and chocolates, Dixie cup icecreams. But wait, what's that? After fifteen minutes of mingling in the foyer, a bell is ringing. Greetings done, gossip exchanged, snacks purchased, people put out their cigarettes, tell each other 'See you after the show', and file inside.

~

Mum books an aisle seat for Dad, the seat next to him for herself. She does this for two reasons. The first is because of his long legs: an aisle seat enables him to swivel his crossed legs into the aisle and be comfortable. The second is so as, should he want to, he can escape from a film he is not interested in or with which he politically disagrees, which, when it comes down to it, is often the same thing.

'God Save the Queen', Australia's national anthem, booms into the theatre. Many people stand, as is required of citizens when the national anthem is played in public places, indoors and out. We Goldblooms are non-standers; refusniks, that's what we are – 'She's not *our* queen' – as are, it transpires, many in this audience, unlike my fellow Saturday matinee crowd. It feels good to be among fellow refusniks, to be not so standout different. '*Goh-hod save our queen.*' It's over. The more compliant patrons seat themselves, everyone settles in.

After the lights dim, the theatre is momentarily completely dark. Then, the massive velvet curtains slowly part and the projector lights up the screen with a silvery shimmer. The film begins.

～

Today, the first of the two films we will see is Sergei Eisenstein's *Ivan the Terrible, Part II*. Stalin admires the character Ivan so there'll be no walking out of this one. Black and white and silent, it is a film filled with intrigues, murder, mayhem: an archetypal scheming woman (an aunt) with the weak son she aspires to have usurp Ivan's throne. Poisonings, plottings. Ivan, the brutal to be kind tsar. It's all there. It's gripping.

At the film's conclusion there is loud applause, not least from me and my viewing companion. What I don't yet understand, given *Ivan* is not in the glorious Technicolor of the musicals so beloved by Bubbeh, is why I am so entranced by this film. I do understand that my admiration has little, if anything, to do with its politics. Also, that there are audience members who are what will come to be called film buffs more than they are political Leftists, though it is not unusual for the two to go hand in hand, at least not in those days. These understandings will come a little later in my life.

At intermission, people begin to stream into the foyer and out onto the street.

'Well,' Dad says as he lights up a cigarette, 'what do you think?'

There it is, a churning in the pit of my stomach. A knot has formed. What if I get it wrong? I would like more time to think about it, but he is waiting for my answer.

'I really liked it,' I reply. Then, before I have a chance to respond to his 'What did you like about it?', a friend greets us and we begin to chat.

The knot begins to uncoil.

〜

Most Sundays of my teenage years, after making him a cup of instant coffee – not too strong, two teaspoons of sugar, a swirl of cream – I am expected to be prepared to give an account of the book he has instructed me the previous Sunday to read, a performance that unnerves me. His choices include authors such as John Steinbeck, Judah Waten, Stefan Zweig, Alan Marshall, Richard Wright and Robert Louis Stevenson. Simone de Beauvoir is the one woman who gets a look in; Dymphna Cusack and Ruth Park I later find by myself.

He repairs to the den, where he waits. After I deliver his coffee, my views and interpretations are to be expounded.

Begin.

〜

An intermission, twenty minutes or so. People who are not staying for the next film leave, while those who arrive in time for it gather around, smoking and talking, drinking coffee, eating. At intermission's end, the same persistent bell announces it's time to return to our seats. In we shuffle.

Throne of Blood next, Akira Kurosawa's interpretation of *Macbeth*, a Shakespeare we are doing at school. Within minutes, Kurosawa's samurai version, also black and white, grips me by the throat, a stranglehold that endures: *Throne of Blood* forever remains in my Top 10.

But wait, what's going on? Fifteen or so minutes after the film begins, people begin to leave, muttering, grumbling; some even boo as they walk up the aisle to the exit. In the flickering light I see two family friends.

'Dad,' I whisper, 'look, there's Ytzhak and Manka.'

They see us too and step aside from the stream of people hastening towards the exit and move close to where Dad is sitting.

'Ytzhak,' Dad whispers, 'where are you going? What's the matter?'

'It's too much, Sam,' Ytzhak replies. 'Ivan *and* Shakespeare? Too much.' He shakes his head. From behind him Manka nods her agreement. 'Too much,' she says.

People around us who remain in their seats begin to shush them.

'We'll see you on the weekend,' says Ytzhak and they leave.

As the screening continues, many people leave. Not us. The Goldblooms remain glued to their seats, transfixed.

As if these two films aren't enough, the 1959 festival is also the year of *The Harp of Burma*, Kon Ichikawa's powerful black and white about the futility of war, which Dad and I also go to see together.

For most of the rest of the festival, Dad shares Mum's ticket with friends (he shares with me again for Alec Guinness as Gulley Jimson in *The Horse's Mouth*, this one in Technicolor). Next year, 1960, although I am still a year younger than the requisite legal age for attendees – eighteen or older unless accompanied by an adult – friends get me a ticket for films I want to see and sneak me in. From 1961, Melbourne Film Festival is a regular on my social calendar.

My love affair with film is to last until my end of days.

In Bandung We Dance the Polka

After a painful and drawn-out illness, Bubbeh dies of cancer on 28 March 1959, which happens to be Mum and Dad's eighteenth wedding anniversary. When the worst of the grief passes – to say nothing of the relief – Mum will say of her domineering mother, 'Trust her to die on our wedding anniversary. I'll bet she did that on purpose.'

Each of Bubbeh's five grandchildren (a sixth is yet to come) is left a legacy of £200. My £200, Dad decides, is to be spent during the January 1960 school holidays to accompany him and two other peace activists, Presbyterian reverend Alf Dickie and Methodist reverend Frank Hartley, to a peace conference in Indonesia. It is my first overseas trip. I am sixteen years old, the envy of my school friends and ready for adventure.

～

Indonesia. The term 'Third World' is not yet commonly used, but at that time, Indonesia is as poor as hell, and is, despite fifteen years of independence, still reeling after four hundred years of Dutch colonialism. It is in Indonesia, Dad believes, I will see living evidence of some of the lessons about poverty, colonialism, imperialism and race he's been drumming into me most of my life.

I digest his politics with my meals. 'See that butter?' In the middle of a meal, Dad points – with his finger, his knife, his fork – to the rippled green glass butter box. 'The price of that butter is set by politics, Sandra.' My sisters look on, silent. I also remain silent. Mum, long-suffering, rolls her eyes. 'Everything is political. The price of butter …'

'Eat your dinner, Sam,' Mum sighs.

Sometimes following his butter lecture, he launches into his story about how, during the Depression (he never uses the adjective 'great'), as a young man, he watches as the ubiquitous 'they' dump oranges off St Kilda Pier into Port Phillip Bay, just, he says, to create scarcity and keep the prices up. Years later, I wonder about this. Why don't growers just dump the oranges into a pit in Mildura or wherever it is in Sunraysia that citrus is grown? Perhaps he meant sellers.

As well, he makes running political commentary on, criticises, revises to his liking, and otherwise makes interjections to *ABC News* – for years to the wireless, and later, with the arrival of television, to the news and, later still, *This Day Tonight*, a behaviour I am to take up myself. While what I most criticise is the newsreader's grammar – I call my tart criticisms editing – I do follow his example and criticise the politics as well.

～

Here I am then, sixteen years old, bright-eyed, vivacious and heading to Indonesia. I am curious about sex but not sure how to go about it.

Pretty sure that my reputation will turn to slut if I am to engage. Still, in Indonesia, I feel sure, I will have an affair. Isn't that what sophisticated people do when they travel overseas?

~

Each year, when Dad departs for another overseas peace conference, most often in Moscow, and later travels elsewhere in Europe, the Middle East or Asia, the whole family piles into the car to accompany him to Essendon Airport, always leaving home much earlier than is necessary because he is afraid he will miss his plane. More recently, with insights gained from years of therapy, I come to wonder about two aspects of these departures. Is his eagerness to leave home, to arrive so early at the airport, more than an expression of his anxiety that the unexpected might occur, causing him to miss his flight? One plausible explanation is that he feels a strong need to escape into a more exciting world than the day to day he lives in, into the world of the politically like-minded, where he doesn't have to deal with his wife, daughters, argumentative and bossy mother-in-law, or his own mother, who comes to lunch every Sunday from Warburton, where she lives, only, for the most part, to sit *shtum* at the table. Or perhaps he looks forward to escaping the routine of his working life.

The other aspect that grows to give me pause is Mum. Why does she never appear to complain about this rush, about having to hang around the airport for a couple of hours before he boards? Mum is terrified of air travel, so she rarely accompanies him. Is it possible she doesn't care to because she finds peace in his absences? Might she have an unconscious desire, a live fantasy, for him to fall out of the sky, to die, so she can start again without him? This fantasy is likely my projection because these are thoughts I had about my own husband, a philanderer just as my father was a philanderer, and a workaholic who seemed rarely to be at home.

Whatever the reason, it means that before the plane carries him away there is a lot of hanging around the airport to be endured.

∽

Here we are now, me and Dad, Mum and my sisters in tow. 'That one,' he says, pointing at a Douglas DC-3 standing nose in the air, tail close to the tarmac, at a slope of about 45 degrees. For the moment its two propellers are idle.

At last the boarding announcement is made. Goodbye hugs and kisses are exchanged. Then he turns to me, grins, puts his arm around my shoulder and says, 'Come on, Sandy. Let's board.' Together we stride towards the waiting plane.

∽

From the moment we land in Java, I am beguiled: thousands of people in the streets are going about their business, trading, eating, riding bicycles, squatting on the footpath smoking, peddling *becaks*. There are thousands of colours, sounds, aromas. Street life is wild, wilder than anything I have seen or will ever see in St Kilda – even in Fitzroy Street, which is probably as wild as it gets in early 1960s Melbourne.

Dewi, a woman quite a bit older than me who speaks perfect English, keeps me company each day. She is my interpreter and translator. It doesn't occur to me at the time, but it's possible she is also my chaperone. Agus, a man also many years older than me – though

I can't be sure and he isn't telling – is smitten with me, and I with him. A peace activist and teachers' trade union official, a delegate to the conference, Agus is short, slim and balding; he has buck teeth and a high-pitched giggle. His heavily accented English isn't too bad. Agus doesn't fit a single physical criterion for a teenage girl's fantasy sweetheart, but he makes me laugh and treats me like an adult. We kiss twice in that month: I still remember the texture of his lips, and that the first time we kiss, our teeth clunk.

~

In our travels around Java – Jakarta, Bandung, Surabaya, Yogyakarta, Solo – I learn alright. I learn that no matter how much he has taught me, what books he's given me to read, the number of harangues, nothing could have prepared me, a girl from a comfortable white middle-class family, for what I see here. Poverty unbearable to witness, a struggle to endure. A mother in a hammock cradles her dead baby. Beggars everywhere – some able-bodied, others maimed and disfigured, sometimes deliberately we are told, in order to beg. A dead man wrapped in newspaper lying in a doorway. The foetid stink of the canal that runs through the centre of Jakarta.

Frequently I gasp with sharp intakes of breath. Sometimes I cry.

Even so, I love it, love everything about it. The street life, the smell of sandalwood, tropical fruits, kerosene and firewood coming from the street stalls where food is being cooked, and the aroma of cloves from the kretek cigarettes. It is so alive, more alive than anywhere I've ever been, than anything I've ever seen, though it must be said that I haven't yet been anywhere much or seen anything much at all, not yet. Sixty years on and the scent of sandalwood incense still evokes old Jakarta.

〜

Rockwiz's Brian Nankervis gives a eulogy at the memorial service for John Pinder, he of the T F Much Ballroom and the Last Laugh Theatre • Restaurant • Zoo.

Nankervis tells the assembled that he grew up in Melbourne's suburban east, wondering if there will be anything more to his life than the dullness of suburbia. One night, a cousin phones to say that his place of work is short staffed. Does the seventeen year old Brian want a job for the night? Nankervis makes his way from his eastern suburbs home to Collingwood.

The moment he walks through the Last Laugh's door, Nankervis recounts, he knows: here it is, the life of which he dreamed. He is overjoyed.

During his eulogy, my thoughts time travel back to Java, to Jakarta. I know exactly the feeling he is talking about.

〜

Dewi – 'Little Goddess' – picks me up at the hotel each morning. On the days Agus comes with us on his way to a conference session, we three go to a market for breakfast: fresh rambutan, red papaya, young coconut, accompanied by a container of coconut rice – foods new and exotic to me. Sometimes we eat at a makeshift table; other times we eat as we wander around. I take in the sights, the sounds, the aromas, while Dewi explains anything I want to know. Decades later, when I see rambutan at Queen Victoria Market for the first time, I am thrilled, plunged into a torrent of fond memories.

After breakfast Dewi and I head off for the rest of our day, to wander the streets, visit temples, to watch batik makers work their craft, sit in cafes, trawl marketplaces.

~

Dewi knows that Australians like to swim, so in Jakarta she takes me to a pool that was a Dutch-only luxury in the colonial years. I am the tallest person there. And the whitest. At the same moment I come out of the change stall, two Indonesian women come out of the stall next to mine. They scream in fright at the sight of me. At night we watch *wayung kulit*, Java's famed shadow-puppet theatre, or go to gamelan concerts; she takes me to visit colleagues, friends and family. In every home, from the wealthiest to the poorest, I am warmly, generously welcomed. Dad, Alf and Frank sometimes come with us. Sometimes, too, Agus.

~

One evening the Australian delegation is invited to dinner at the home of the Minister for Education, an Indonesian-born Chinese man. There, we are served a sumptuous feast of many courses. Nothing about this meal could be further removed from the over-cooked Sunday night Chinese dinner we sometimes have at home. We buy the meals from a Chinese cafe in nearby Glenferrie Road. In these early days of takeaway, in a time before plastic containers, Mum and I, or one of Sister Two or Sister Three, gather up several lidded saucepans of different sizes and drive to the cafe, a plain shop with green Laminex tables down the middle of the room and booth seating against one wall. We order three or four of the family's favourite dishes: chicken and almonds, chicken chow mien that comes with a paper bag filled with crispy fried noodles, sweet and sour somethingorother and special fried rice. The vegetables are pale, the greens overcooked, the sauces gluggy. But the noodles and the almonds are crunchy, so that – along with all that delectable salt – is good enough for us.

At the minister's house, the food is vibrant, every dish beautifully fresh and aromatic, the ingredients differentiated. The Glenferrie Road sweet and sour fish bears no resemblance to the dish of the same name the servants place on the table. Not even the meals we eat on special occasions at the erstwhile Fairy Stork in Acland Street come close.

At the minister's house, I learn to use chopsticks.

~

The conference sessions aren't of much interest to me, but I do attend the closing night grand gala. Scores of circular dinner tables set with elegant crockery and cutlery on fine linen fill a cavernous room, which has a dance floor and a band shell where twenty musicians attired in military uniform sit quietly talking, smoking kreteks, awaiting their cue. The Australian delegation sits with Dewi and five or six people from other parts of the world. Agus is at a table with comrade trade unionists.

Once again, dinner is a sumptuous multicourse affair. Between courses, when the band strikes up a waltz, a polka, a tango and every now and again some 1940s swing, people get up from their seats to dance.

Next, the band strikes up a polka.

'Come on, Sandy,' Dad says, grinning, as he stands up from the table, his hand outstretched. 'Let's show 'em how it's done.'

Among the many Indonesians and the handful of Westerners, Dad and I are standout tall. He is six foot three; I am just shy of five foot eleven. We clomp our way around the dance floor until the band comes to a halt. Dad returns me to our table and is about to go to find himself another dance partner when a military man, his uniform lavishly bedecked with gold braid and medals, walks across the room to us. He is President Sukarno's aide. 'The president invites your daughter to dance,' he says to Dad, then turns towards me, bows and nods. I look across the room at President Sukarno, Indonesia's adored Bung Karno (Brother Karno), leader of the Indonesian independence struggle and the independent nation's first president. Sukarno makes a barely discernible nod in my direction.

Dad gives his permission. The military man leads me across the room to the president. Even in my stockinged feet I would be a bit taller than the Indonesian president, though this seems not to bother him and it doesn't bother me. Having always felt flat footed on the dance floor, I am more concerned with the quality of my dancing. Besides, he's wearing his traditional cap, his *songkok*, which gives him additional height.

The band is playing a waltz. Rock'n'roll and bebop jazz, my main musical pleasures, seem to have not yet found their way to Indonesia – at least not to this function.

The Indonesian president and the Australian teenager have little to say to each other.

'Are you enjoying yourself in our country?'

'Yes, thank you, I am enjoying myself.'

'Yes, I am still at school.'

49

'Yes, two sisters.'

What does a sixteen year old girl know about how to converse with a president? I have bupkis.

Sukarno twirls me around the dance floor. His hold is firm, his step light. I begin to relax.

In time, the music comes to a halt. The president thanks me, and the aide-de-camp delivers me back to my father, where Alf, Dad and some other conference delegates sit smoking (the Methodist Frank Hartley does not smoke or drink), engaged in earnest conversation.

'How did you go?' Dad asks, grinning. 'You looked pretty good out there.'

'Did I? I was nervous,' I reply. 'I didn't know what to say to him. Besides, I've got two left feet.'

'You did fine,' he says, though I'm not altogether reassured.

⁓

That night I dream that Dad and I are strolling with Dewi in a Jakarta marketplace when he slips on a rambutan pip. He flies up in the air, then falls with a thud on top of a pile of fruit peelings and rambutan pips. His head cracks open; he dies.

At the moment he dies, I wake up and realise I'm laughing. This dream intrigues me because usually when I'm killing him off – which is not infrequent in my teenage years – the dreams are terrifyingly murderous, arson-filled dreams about him – or me – burning up in the flames of hell; there is always agonising screams. I wake from these dreams drenched in sweat. The night of the rambutan-pip dream? No fear. No sweat.

⁓

When Agus and I kiss goodbye, our teeth don't clunk.

Dewi, Agus and I all promise to write, but not much correspondence passes between us: a dwindling exchange of cards, fewer letters. It is not too long before what little exchange there has been between us becomes silence.

Late in 1965, after the Suharto putsch, word reaches us via the international peace movement grapevine that Agus is in prison; Dewi has vanished. Then in 1966, the Melbourne peace movement office learns that Agus and Dewi are dead – murdered, it is presumed. Everyone I met there is dead or missing, presumed dead. They, along with a million others (some reports say as many as three million), have been slaughtered in the sweep of Suharto's Right-wing military coup. Theirs is a fate much worse than dying after slipping on a rambutan pip.

White Knight Rescue

At seventeen, my desire to go to art school thwarted by Mum – 'You'll never make a living doing that nonsense' – I am packed off to a local typing school. Once I learn where the keys are located on the manual typewriter, the teacher covers my hands with a tea towel to teach me touch typing. 'No peeping,' she instructs. Keys are to be struck in time to Johann Strauss' *Radetzky March*: *Oom poomp oom poomp oom poomp duddle* … in the 4/4 time common to military marches.

As my familiarity with and skills on the keyboard improve, my teacher increases the tempo of the music. In short time, my typing is so fast that the key levers are forever sticking to one another, jamming in a bunch. Because the keys can't keep up with me, I have to slow my pace.

Several years will pass before the IBM Selectric, aka the golf ball, and other electric typewriters are introduced into Australian offices.

For now, though, typing test given, typing test passed. Time to look for a job.

～

I scour *The Age* employment section, where I find a secretarial job in a St Kilda Road office on the bend where Toorak Road West meets St Kilda Road. My place of work is on the ground floor of a double storey Victorian house, one in a row of several converted to offices. On the Toorak Road side of this rounded corner is a group of shops, including a cafe. I would rather be in the city, but I haven't found anything there that appeals, and because I have no shorthand nothing is offered, so I settle. At the end of the interview, the boss asks if I can start in the morning.

Next morning, my hair is teased and smoothed over into a beehive, Max Factor pancake makeup smoothed on, matte orangey-red lipstick and black eyeliner perfectly applied. My dress is ironed, and crumpled newspaper is packed into the toes of my winklepicker flatties. I am ready for my first day at work.

~

Typing, filing, answering the phone, fetching morning tea, lunch and afternoon tea for the boss, more typing, and transcribing his letters from a dictaphone. So goes my first working day. When I arrive home, Dad says, 'How was it?' Mum is standing close by, listening. My account goes thus: I am happy to be there, happy that I'm earning my own wage and that I will be paid at the end of the week. Happy to know, I tell them without boasting, that from the start I am good at my work.

'See, I told you you'd enjoy it,' Mum says.

I don't let her see me scowl.

Board is to be paid. Although the charge is minimal – around 7.5 per cent of my wage – I protest. My parents explain that paying

53

my way is a good lesson to learn because when I leave home, I will have to pay rent to a landlord and shopkeepers for food. 'Might as well get used to it.'

'It's not because we need the money,' says Mum.

Unbeknown to me, Mum socks away my board money together with my school banking money, the sum total of which she gives me in the form of a cheque a few days before Jack and I marry. Several hundred pounds of it, accumulated over eight years of weekly school banking together with the four years of board. Impressive.

~

And so it goes, or similarly, for another week or two, until things begin to change.

'How was work today?' His question has become customary.

'Fine,' I reply, with limited enthusiasm.

In an instant he knows that the day has not been at all fine. 'Sure?'

'Yeah, Dad, sure.'

Every day for a full week my reply becomes increasingly unenthusiastic, almost surly, until finally he insists I tell him what's upsetting me. 'Out with it,' he says.

I can feel myself burning with embarrassment, with shame. 'The boss … he … he … touches …' My face is aflame. I want to be tapped on the shoulder by a magic wand and *poof*, disappeared.

Patiently, Dad waits. When it's clear I'm not going to say anything more, he says, 'Tell you what, Sanny. How about I take you to work tomorrow, hmm?'

'Do I have to go?'

'Let's just go together and see how we go. OK?'

'OK,' I sniffle. I don't want to go to work, but without having any notion of what it will be I know something big is going to happen. There's going to be trouble.

~

After breakfast, we drive to my workplace.

Surprised to see me arrive accompanied, the boss says, an enquiring look on his face, 'This must be your dad, Sandra,' and proffers his hand. 'How are you, Mr …'

Before he has a chance to complete his sentence, Dad, who does not put out his hand, interrupts. 'My daughter tells me you've been touching her up.'

Right there, on that spot, I want to die.

'What? No, no …' The boss looks aggrieved, but I can see there is something else. It's there, in his eyes. Fear.

'My daughter wouldn't lie about something like that.'

The boss is beginning to look sheepish. He retrieves his hand, wipes the palm on his trousers and shuffles slightly from one foot to the other. 'But …'

'No buts,' Dad says. His tone is more stern than I've ever heard it. 'If you don't want me to report you to the police, you'll listen to me. Now, this is what's going to happen. Effective immediately, Sandra will leave your employ. You will write out a cheque for six weeks severance pay for her right now. What's more,' his voice becomes menacing – more menacing – 'I'm going to keep an eye on you, and if I ever hear that you are making advances on any other girls who come to work here, you'll be in big strife.' Finishing with a flourish, he says, 'You're damned lucky I don't job you one.'

Despite my embarrassment, my overwhelming desire is to giggle at the notion of Dad jobbing my boss. Overjoyed as I am with Dad's white knight performance, I'm pretty sure there is no way he can monitor what the boss does to his future female staff. Still, if Dad's words put the wind up that man for even an hour or two, even just for this moment, I'm thrilled.

~

Dad has a word with family friends, who offer me employment in their Collins Street travel agency. During my lunch hour I join some of my friends who work in the city, mostly people who I meet at Jazz Centre 44 on weekends. During the working week we hang out on the corner of Collins Street and the Australia Arcade, which runs alongside the now demolished Hotel Australia. On that corner, we lean up against the wall while we eat our sandwiches, drink milk-shakes or fizzy drinks and smoke cigarettes. We plan our weekends at Jazz Centre 44, the beach, the movies, and talk about what we did the week before, what we're reading.-

This is the life.

'How was work today, Sandy?' Dad peers at me over the top of *The Herald*, which he lowers in order to see my face.

Grinning broadly, I reply in the hipster speak of the day: 'It was a gas, Dad. Really groovy.'

Never again is there any need to go accompanied to work.

What the Psychologist Says

'Hello, Mummy,' I say as I stroll into my parents' house one sunny afternoon. It is unusual that I call her this. For most of our lives, my sisters and I call our parents by their given names: 'Hello, Rosie,' 'Hello Sammy.'

Mum blushes with pleasure. 'Oooh,' she squeaks. 'Mummy.'

'Hello Da …'

He chops me off at the pass. 'Don't you dare.'

'… addy.'

'I said don't.'

'OK.'

'I don't like it.'

'Al*right*.'

By the time I stop calling my mother Rosie and take up Mum I am already fifty. Clearly, she is pleased. Dad holds fast, but in time, while backing away from the childish Daddy, I begin to call him Dad; he desists from objection. Only when I want to get up his nose do I call him Daddy. When I do, a thunderous rumbling of annoyance begins, then, after a while, it blows over.

~

Another sunny afternoon, some months later. I arrive to visit at the same time as a family friend, Esther the psychologist. Esther is about halfway between me and my parents in age. I am very fond of her. She is lively, smart and lots of fun. She always looks as if she's just stepped off the page of a fashion magazine, albeit in a casual kind of way.

Greetings all around.

'Tea, everyone?'

'No thanks, Mum. Not for me. How are you today, Dad?'

Esther spins towards me. 'You called them Mum and Dad,' she exclaims.

'Yes?'

'About bloody time,' says Esther.

'About what time?'

'Time that you are prepared to acknowledge your relationships … that these people' – she sweeps her arm around in an arc to encompass both parents – 'are your parents, not your friends.'

It's been a year since I commenced therapy so immediately I understand what Esther is talking about.

'What do you think?' Esther asks.

For a moment I don't answer, then: 'I like it, Esther, I do.'

'What about you, Rosa?'

'I like it too,' Mum says shyly, 'very much.'

Esther grins at Dad. 'What about you, Sam?'

'She'd better not call me Daddy,' he grumps.

We three women laugh.

Mum brings her special biscuits out of the pantry. Dad moves his head from side to side in one of his damned if I know what the hell is going on here shakes, but before he turns towards his seat, away from where Esther and I are standing, I see the beginnings of a smile.

It has taken me forty years to start calling my parents Mum and Dad. I continue to call them that for the rest of their lives.

~

My daughter, for all the fraught in our relationship, only ever calls me Mum or Ma. Even when I offer – ask – her to call me Sandra, she refuses. I become glad she never takes up my offer.

My son only ever calls me Sandra, and although twice in his adult life I ask if he will call me Mum or Ma or something that indicates I'm his mother, he has always turned me down.

Can't win 'em all.

Lunch

Arteriosclerosis, doctor says. Arteries full of mush, the result of a lifelong diet of rich Jewish food, of chocolate and lolly gobbling, of smoking. Needs to go on a diet, doctor says. Pritikin. 'See that?' Doctor Mac slaps himself on the stomach and invites us to observe what Pritikin has done for him.

Mum and I gaze at Doctor Mac's hand as it rests on his firm, flat stomach. The ring on his pinky finger is a large carved gold band (probably 24 carat) with an inlaid cut ruby. Beneath the fine cotton of his shirt there appears to be no evidence of flab. Not a skerrick. If a Flattest Abs in the Hospital contest were to be held, Doctor Mac would win. Hands down. But I'm not as interested in the state of his abs as I am in the gleam in his eyes.

He must have a lover. Probably has. Two of the nurses tell us Dr Mac and his wife have separated.

'Pritikin,' Doctor Mac repeats, wagging a finger at Mum, encouraging and admonishing in equal measure. Through the blanket, he grabs Dad's toe, wiggles it, waves an airy goodbye to everyone in the room and strides off, though not before glancing at himself in the mirror – a little longer than might be considered modest – and beaming with pleasure at the reflection he sees there.

Already Mum looks anguished. She knows what this means, even if Dad doesn't. Pritikin, she understands, is American for deprivation. Goodbye salt. Goodbye oil, goodbye chicken schmaltz. Goodbye fat-rimmed rump steak with chips. Farewell chopped liver. Goodbye to all that food she loves. Goodbye sugar, butter and cream, the foods he loves.

Already – I imagine – she is plotting her way around how to slip some salt into the soup, some oil into an otherwise dreary stirfry. Can she get away with grilling a piece of marbled steak once in a while? Roasting a leg of lamb with the crisp, fatty bits left on? She could give him the lean. Mrs Sprat and her husband Jack. How on earth can she possibly stop him from eating liquorice allsorts, soft sugary jubes and Cherry Ripes? What about the Malt'O'Milk biscuits slathered with butter?

～

Mum buys all the books: Australian Pritikin, American Pritikin. There's even a Chinese Pritikin: stirfries cooked in water or clear vegetable stock, steamed vegetables with low-salt soy sauce, tofu this, tofu that. She buys the Chinese edition. 'Gawd,' she says contemptuously, 'it all looks like crap to me.'

～

Even though they've been married for fifty years, she doesn't reckon on his determination, his iron will to live. If the renunciation of

61

pleasure is what it takes to hang on for a few more years, renunciation it's going to be.

He does it in fine style.

To everyone's surprise, Dad is an immediate convert. In no time at all, he comes to love unsalted vegetables, grilled or poached fish and chicken breast (no crispy skin, no salt, no schmaltz). He learns to love cakes made with ... he has no idea what cakes are made with, but he loves every item she bakes. He allows himself the smallest portion – no butter, no cream ('Thank you, dear, I'd better not') – and with every mouthful, usually at afternoon tea, he tilts his head to one side, puckers his lips into a little kiss, shuts his eyes and hums, 'Mmmm, dee-licious.' Then he takes a large gulp of tea with skim milk – or none – and washes it down.

Mum looks as if she'd like to strangle him.

Fresh fruit becomes his favourite dessert. 'Lovely banana,' he says without so much as a trace of irony. Mum looks up from the miserable whatever it is on her plate to stare at him. No, not even a hint of a smile. There he sits, chewing his banana (his apple, his pear) to mush. When he's finished, he raises his hands in the air and shakes his fingers about as if he is limbering up to play the piano. Mum leans across the table and passes him a serviette; he stops playing the piano and wipes his hands. 'Beautiful.' Satisfied, he sighs, and then adds, 'Good onya, Rosie.'

Under her breath, Mum mutters, '*Drek*. All of it. Crap.'

This performance – or a variation of it – will be re-enacted after many a meal for the next eight years.

～

Each bed in a four-bed ward is occupied by an elderly gentleman. One of them is Dad.

An assortment of newer ailments, complementary to his cardio-vascular range, brings him in again. Among them, an increasing and disturbing tendency to fall asleep in the middle of a meal, often while chewing his food, a side effect of several of his medications. More disconcerting still, he begins to fall asleep at the wheel while driving the car. One day, driving home along Kooyong Road, he nods off and swerves into a lamppost. He is not hurt, but the damage to the car is such that it is written off. No longer permitted to drive, his licence revoked, his depression increases manyfold.

Also troubling, Pritikin notwithstanding, his cholesterol count continues to climb.

Poor circulation in his feet causes him pain.

Pangs in his chest from angina.

Malfunctioning from head to toes.

⁓

I have come to visit him.

When I arrive, his face is tilted up towards the overhead television screen. Martina Hingis is three points away from winning the Sydney International tennis championship. Momentarily, he turns to greet me: 'Hello, Sandy,' he says, then, before I have a chance to reply, he puts one finger to his lips, points another to the screen and says, 'Sssshhh. Won't be long now.'

Dad's dinner tray looks dismal. Greater limitations are placed on his meals because now, a gall bladder infection has been added to his list of ailments, as has medication-induced diabetes. Wholemeal bread crusts, left in disarray on a white china plate that bears the hospital logo, are all that remain of a sandwich. Glistening yellow jelly, a sunny mound of perfectly cut cubes nestled in a clear glass bowl, remains, surprisingly, untouched.

'One championship point,' Dad says, as he stares at his overhead screen.

'She's going to make it, Sam,' the gentleman in the bed next to Dad predicts.

'Looks like,' Dad agrees. 'Two championship points.'

Dad's teacup has been drained. A plastic tub of hermetically sealed apple juice has not been touched. There is no sign of the two shortbread biscuits that are usually served with tea or coffee, nor of the cellophane wrap they come in.

'Three championship points.'

'It's Martina's match. Can't lose now.'

'Looks like.'

Bored, I remove my gaze to the Dandenong Ranges, dark against the cloudless early evening sky.

Thwock, grunt and … *thththwock*! The crowd goes wild. Hingis goes wild.

'Game, set and championship,' says Dad in unison with commentator Fred Stolle. 'G'day, Sandy,' he says, this time smiling as he turns his face towards me to be kissed.

'Hello, Dad. Good match?' I kiss his stubbled cheek.

'What did I tell you?' The neighbour alongside is satisfied, though not smug. 'Want my biscuit?' he enquires of the gentleman diagonally opposite Dad. 'Go on, have it,' he urges. 'I'm not allowed.' A doleful grimace fails to hide his grin. 'Here girlie, pass it to him, will you?'

I smile at his cheekiness, do his bidding and return to sit beside Dad.

Together we stare at the advertisements on the screen until my neck begins to ache. While Dad continues to watch, I cast my eyes over this evening's dinner menu. The sandwich filling, I learn, was corned beef and salad, probably some tomato, lettuce, a bit of grated carrot, a slice or two of cucumber. No butter, no mayonnaise, no mustard. Oh yes, looks as if there might have been a slice of tinned beetroot.

'A breakfast menu for you, Mr Goldbloom.' A man from catering places the menu on the trolley alongside unopened tubs of juice and jelly.

Dad sighs.

I glance at the man's nametag: Javier. Javier says, 'Louise will be along soon to collect it.' Then, 'Enjoy your evening.' Javier smiles munificently and leaves.

The receding squeak of Javier's rubber soles on the vinyl floor can still be heard when the dietician arrives. Smiling, Louise places her clipboard on the trolley. 'You've got your breakfast menu, Mr G? No rush,' she says with a smile. 'When you're ready.'

'I have no idea what to mark.' Dad is petulant. 'I'm not allowed to eat anything.'

Dad tells Louise that a meal delivered earlier is whipped away before he has a chance to eat any of it. The corners of his mouth turn down. 'They brought me this instead.' He indicates the jelly with his chin. 'Not much in that.'

Patiently smiling, Louise says, 'And a corned beef and salad sandwich. Well, this menu is for tomorrow, Mr G. Don't you worry, we'll work it out together later.' She pats his hand.

Despondent, Dad nods. Louise leaves.

'What about a jelly bean?' I offer, even though I know it's taboo.

He loves jelly beans – though not black ones. Our family plays the game of Jelly Beans Are Good For You, a fiction that gains broad currency in the 1950s, probably derived from the word 'glucose' on the packet and the fact they are sold in pharmacies.

He perks up, nods with childlike enthusiasm. 'Yes, please, Sandy, that would be lovely,' and, just before I walk out the door, 'Don't tell your mother.'

I scoot down three flights of terrazzo stairs, stride through the foyer to the pharmacy and return in the lift with the jelly beans. On my return, I notice he's eaten the jelly cubes.

He tears open the packet with his teeth, pours its contents onto the trolley, picks out the black ones and offers them to me. I scoop them out of his palm and pop one into my mouth. *Chew chew chew.* Then the next. *Chew chew ch …*

'What did you have for lunch?' he asks as each of us chews away, nodding his thanks for the sweets.

'Lunch?' I echo, surprised. It is not like him to ask about his daughter's – or anyone's – meal menus. He prefers to see me and Mum as the eaters in our family. He deludes himself that he is a victim of Mum's force feeding, though I suppose there's an element of this that's true enough.

'Lunch,' he insists. 'What did you have?'

'Salad and pasta.'

'At home?'

'No, Dogs Bar.' We have eaten there together many times.

'What sort of salad?'

'Radicchio, rocket, cos lettuce …'

He wrinkles his nose; bitter leaves don't appeal to him.

'Was it a nice dressing?'

'Yes, it was. Simple, fresh.'

'What sort?'

'Lemon juice and olive oil. Salt. Pepper.'

'That's all? No garlic?'

'Just lemon juice and oli …'

'No tomato? No other vegetables?'

'No.'

He shakes his head. 'Your mother puts in …'

'I know, Dad, everything.'

'The works.' He nods emphatically and smiles.

'And?'

'And what?'

'What sort of pasta?'

I describe a dish of fettuccini, tomatoes, basil, parmigiano.

'Coffee?'

'Of course,' I retort.

'With dessert? Cake?'

I cough self-consciously. 'Well …'

Impatient for my answer, he waves away my discomfort. 'Never mind your bloody diabetes. What did you have?'

'What's this about, Dad?'

'What sort of cake?' The pink tip of his tongue slowly appears, just visible as he licks the corner of his mouth.

'Tarte tatin …' I hesitate, then, abandoning all inhibition, I confess, 'with cream.'

'The thick one? From Whatsitsname Island?'

'King. Yes, so thick you could stand …'

'… a spoon in it.'

Satisfied, he settles deeper into his pillows and smiles.

Is that a dribble of saliva leaking from the corner of his mouth? It *is*!

'Dad …?'

Without so much as a hint of self-consciousness, he licks the corner of his mouth, smiles and, with his long, pale index finger pressed against his lips, brightly chimes, 'News time.' He flips the channel to the ABC, turns up the volume and returns his attention to the screen.

I sit through the headlines, then stand and walk to the window. Night has fallen. Below, stretching for miles out to the east, lights twinkle against the navy sky. A number 5 tram rattles along Wattletree Road, on its way to the city.

By the time I return to Dad's bedside, the broadcaster is pointing at the weather map. Dad is watching intensely. Why, I wonder, would a man who will be bed-bound for at least another week be so interested in the weather? Because this is how it has always been, from that day in 1956 when our family acquires a television set, just in time to watch the Olympic Games.

~

Me and my sisters have been nagging Mum and Dad to buy a television set. 'Yankee rubbish,' is his most common response. 'Not having that crap in my house.'

Then, one day, after months of relentless pleading being met by dogged refusal and critiques of US cultural imperialism, we arrive home from school to find all the lounge-room furniture rearranged into a semicircle facing into a corner of the room. Our Astor console television arrives to greetings of near hysterical glee, just in time for us to watch The Mickey

Mouse Club *that night, and to watch the Melbourne Olympic Games soon after. Despite his protestations about US cultural crap, his two most adored programs?* Westerns: Gunsmoke *and* Have Gun – Will Travel. *Oh, and* ABC News. *Under no circumstances are any of these programs to be missed or ever interrupted.*

~

The next day when I go to visit, only a glass of water is on his table.

'How are you today, Dad?'

He looks glum. *'Azoy,'* he replies. 'So-so. How about you?'

We exchange pleasantries for a while, talk a little about the state of the world, which he considers to be parlous.

'Did you bring the jelly beans?'

It hasn't occurred to me that I am to make a daily offering. Once again I go down the stairs, buy a packet, return to the ward and place them on the trolley. Once again he tears open the packet with his teeth, sets the black ones aside and starts gobbling the other colours.

'How was your lunch today, Dad? Better?'

'So-so,' he says again. He looks at me over the rim of his spectacles. 'How was yours?' Expectation fills his voice; it is in his gaze.

Oh no, are we going to do the mouthful by mouthful again?

Seems we are.

And so it goes. Describing the lunch I'd eaten before coming to see him, or what I might be planning for dinner that night. Recounting becomes part of many of my visits, though I never volunteer; I always make him ask. With each description his tongue peeps a little further out of his mouth, followed by a surreptitious but increasingly obvious licking of his chops.

After several of these recitations I become aware of a change in what I order in cafes, in how I prepare my meals. On days when I'm going to visit him, if I cook, I realise I often prepare for myself those foods he likes best. When I eat out, I make sure I have at least one dish he enjoys, including – perhaps especially – dessert. Now, when the performance of our ritual begins, I can feed him what he once loved and is now denied.

Between the jelly beans delivery and the menu recitations, Dad seems satisfied, pleased even. I deliver my father these fantasy feeds – and a small packet of jelly beans – most days of the six that remain until the end of this hospital admission.

Oh, what a good daughter am I.

M—

Open heart surgery is required. A date is set. My father sounds apprehensive when he tells me the surgery will leave him with a scar from his neckline to his *pipik*, his belly button. I do my best to reassure him that everything will be alright, to little avail.

~

At the time of the impending heart surgery, I'm dating M—, a sweet man with a generous spirit, a charming remnant of a Polish accent, a love of late night phone calls and – I am soon to realise – a coke habit. We meet at The Continental, a cafe and music venue on Greville Street in Prahran, where I have come to listen to saxophonist Gary Bartz.

M— is the son of Holocaust survivors. Soon after we meet, M— tells me that during the Holocaust, he and his parents survive because they are fair haired and blue eyed and so are able to pass as Christians; his parents raise him to believe he is Catholic. After the family emigrates to and settles in Melbourne, M— is enrolled in a state school, where he teams up with the antisemitic boys who beat up Jewish kids. One day, when he is about twelve, M— comes home from school with a black eye. When his mother asks what happened, he tells her, 'I was in a fight with a dirty Yid. He beat me up.'

M—'s mother slaps him across the face, then says in a tone he has never before heard, 'Never let me hear you say that again. Now I'm going to tell you. You?' she says. 'You yourself are a Yid, M—. Yes, you are. You are Jewish.'

He tells me how shocked he is to hear this, how afraid he is that his bullyboy friends will find out and beat the shit out of him.

Find out they do. As M— anticipates, his former friends beat the shit out of him: punches, kicks, to say nothing of constant derision, taunting and humiliation.

~

When I tell M— I can't meet him for lunch tomorrow because I'm going to see Dad before his surgery, he is disappointed, but offers to drive me to the hospital anyway. 'I'll show Sam my scar so he won't be scared.'

M— and Dad have not yet met. I fear that M—'s exuberance might be too much for Dad in his nervous pre-op state. But I smile all the same. Of course I have seen M—'s scar, which he refers to as his zipper. Even though a couple of years have passed since his heart surgery, the dark red flesh where the incision was made still looks raw.

'Alright,' I say. 'Thanks.'

We find a park and make our way to Dad's single-bed ward. He starts to smile as I enter the room, but then he sees M— and his smile slips a little. 'You must be M—.'

'Hello, Sam.'

They shake hands. M— steps up. He reassures Dad that everything will be fine, that he shouldn't worry. Already I see that this is too much for Dad, especially from a stranger. M— continues to wax reassuring. Then, as he comes to his denouement, he says, 'See?' and rips open the steel studs of his check shirt: *snap snap snap snap snap*.

Dad is aghast. 'Oh, no. Please, no,' he says, holding up a hand to shield himself from the sight of M—'s scar. 'Not now, please.'

Would any time have been alright? Unlikely.

Although I want to stay, I feel I should take M— and leave. But, satisfied that he's performed another good deed (the first being to drive me to the hospital), M— smiles grandly at Dad, wishes him well in Yiddish – 'Sei gesunt, Shmuel' – turns to me and says, 'I'll leave you to be with your father. I'll wait for you downstairs. Don't rush. I'll be fine.' M— does up his shirt studs and leaves the room.

Dad is shaking his head. 'Too much, Sandy,' he says. 'Too much.'

'It was, Dad, and I'm sorry, but he meant only kindness,' I reply. 'He wanted to reassure you.'

Relenting, Dad chuckles. We grin at each other. I sit on the chair beside his bed and we talk for a while. Twenty minutes later, a nurse enters the room. It is clear that she has business here, so I get up from the chair, give him a hug, wish him good luck with the surgery, and leave. My chest feels tight.

～

After what feels like a very long night, the morning of the surgery dawns. Mum wants to wait at the hospital until the surgery is over, so the four of us – me, Mum and my sisters – make our way there.

We go to the canteen where we sit for a while drinking coffee, making listless conversation. From time to time, Sister Three and I step out to a space in the hospital garden where it's permitted to smoke. Sometimes we go together, sometimes alone.

Mum becomes agitated; she wants to go to the ICU waiting room, just in case the nurse needs to find us and doesn't know where we are, so we make our way there and sit for quite some time.

A theatre nurse eventually comes to tell us that the surgery went well and that Dad, still unconscious from the anaesthetic, is being taken to the intensive care unit to recover. The duty nurse will call us when we can go in to see him.

After more time – how long? – we see him being wheeled into the ICU, but we have to wait a while before we are permitted to go in there. When that time comes, the nurse tells us we are too many to all go in together, so it is agreed that Mum and I will be first in.

All puffy-looking and groggy, he is barely conscious.

A nurse who is holding a phone approaches. 'Are you Sandra? There's a Dr Feinstein on the phone for you.'

Do not grin, I urge myself. Do not. I know it's M—, but what is he up to?

'Hello, doctor,' I say. 'Kind of you to call.'

'How's Sam?'

'Groggy, but he's going to be OK.'

'I'll see you tonight.'

'You will. Thanks for calling, doctor.'

M—'s call delights me. We hang up and I hand the phone back to the ICU nurse. Tonight I will see him, a pleasure to look forward to.

⌒

In couplets – me and Mum, Sisters Two and Three – we take turns to sit with Dad for a while in the recovery room. Then, it's time to go home. We are all exhausted. 'See you tomorrow,' I say to the others.

It is around four o'clock when I get home. Just as I open my apartment door, the phone rings. It is the hospital. A nurse says her name, but as soon as she says it I forget what it is. Quite possibly I don't hear it at all. What I can hear is my blood pumping, my heart pounding.

'Sandra, you had better come now. Your dad is fading fast.'

'But I left less than an hour …'

'He crashed,' she says. 'If you want to see him, come now. He might not make it.'

The Americans have a saying: You can't push the river. Today, the river takes the form of peak-hour traffic and you cannot push peak-hour traffic, not anywhere. From North Fitzroy to Malvern, the off-peak drive usually takes around forty minutes, forty-five tops; that is not going to happen this afternoon. Well, no point getting agitated. I buckle my seatbelt and settle in. To distract me from the traffic and from my anxiety, I put on my Yiddish 101 tape.

Driving along Nicholson Street, it crosses my mind that I haven't called M— to let him know I'm going to have to postpone our date. I will call from the payphone at the hospital.

As I begin my journey south across the river, an all-enveloping calm, as light as gossamer, settles on me.

~

'I've decided to learn Yiddish,' I announce to my parents.

Mum is delighted. 'Good on you, Sandy,' she says, smiling.

Mum and Bubbeh spoke Yiddish together and often with their friends, but neither of them teach me or my sisters the language. Yiddish was their secret women's business language, the language they used to bitch about Dad, to gossip about their friends and family members, to worry about the children – especially that naughty, rebellious daughter, Sandra.

'Smart move,' says Dad.

'Smart?'

In response to my quizzical look, he replies, 'You enjoy travelling, yes?' I nod. 'Well, there are Jews in every country in the world, so no matter what the language of the country you're in, if you ever get into strife or need help, you'll find a local synagogue and you'll be right.'

Smart thinking, Dad.

∼

More than an hour passes before I reach the hospital. Relieved to find a nearby parking space, I rush straight to the ICU. Mum, Sisters Two and Three are already in the room: Mum and Two stand on one side of the bed, Three on the other. I stand at the bed's end. Dad, wearing an oxygen mask, is moaning and thrashing about. At first, my attention is drawn to the wide bore tubing that comes out of – or does it go into? – a clear plastic mask secured by lengths of green elastic strapped around each ear. Struggling to keep from laughing, my first thought on seeing him hooked up to this paraphernalia that comes off his face is: *Oh, look, it's Babar the Elephant.*

A nurse enters the room, which throws a wet blanket over my mirth.

'Does he know we're here?'

'We don't know that,' the nurse replies, 'but it might help if you say encouraging things to him, urge him on to come out of this slide.'

So we begin to urge him on, as if he were a one-man footy team, or a racehorse.

'Come on, Dad, you can do it.'

'Come on, Dad, you're going to make it.'

And, Mum, most tenderly, 'Come on, Sammy. I want you to come home.'

None of it seems to work, not even when we raise our voices, the better for him to hear us above his own loud moans. He continues to thrash about.

'For chrissake, Three,' I say. 'Try some of your Buddhist breathing stuff on him.'

Sister Three lays on hands, touches his brow, holds his hand, speaks in a low soothing voice, encourages him to breathe slowly, calmly. 'In … out … slowly. That's the way, Sammy.' She repeats it, instructs him, encourages him, over and over, over and over.

Behold, he begins to settle. His breathing becomes steadier, then becomes calm.

From that moment on, Mum will say, 'We saved him, didn't we? We saved his life.'

Maybe we all did, but I like to think it was Three and her meditative ways that did the trick.

～

Years after he dies, Mum and I sit in her car parked in front of my apartment block. She tells me that after this surgical episode, to alleviate his pain, there is a period of self-administering pethidine through an IV.

77

As a result he soon develops a dependence on it, too much so for Mum and his doctor's liking. The doctor, Mum tells me, puts him on a diminishing course of methadone and books him some appointments with a psychologist.

Here it is again, a story untold. Was he ashamed? Embarrassed that he developed a drug habit? Uncomfortable that, after all his railing against the talking cure, he not only finds partaking – might he use the word 'indulging'? – in it helpful but also, according to Mum, that it does him some good.

While my curiosity about what he might have divulged to the therapist is boundless, it is never to be satisfied.

∼

Mum and the sisters go home to Mum's; I go to my apartment. Just after nine o'clock, M— phones. Towards the end of our short conversation, he offers to bring me something to eat. He hears my hesitation. 'Don't worry. We'll just eat together. I won't stay.'

Sitting facing each other on the couch, we eat together. Between mouthfuls M— asks about Dad and again reassures me that he'll be alright. He clears away the empty containers, the bowls and chopsticks.

'Come on,' he says.

'What?'

'You're going to have a bath, and then I'm going to put you to bed.'

M— runs the bath, pours in Epsom salts, drops in a couple of splashes of aromatic oil. I slide in. As the water envelops me, I think about a line from Don DeLillo's *Underworld*. The author has one of his characters, a man in his sixties who is sitting in his bath, say: 'Nothing fits the body so well as water.' In this moment, I know nothing could be more true.

M— scrubs my back and washes me; he dries me off and helps me into my nightie. My exhaustion, physical as well as emotional, is so deep that not a single erotic spark emanates from his touch. Then, as he said he would, M— puts me to bed, leaves me with a joint I don't smoke, strokes my hair, kisses me goodnight and leaves.

∼

After the night of being bathed and put to bed by M—, the time between our meeting, between our late-night phone conversations, grows longer and still longer.

'What's going on?' I ask M—. After several such enquiries, M— tells me he has continued to see his wife while dating me. He tells me he begged her to take him back. He just has to go back, he says. How could he not? Sex with her is sensational.

The night of this declaration, the revelation of his deception, is the last time M— and I see each other. I continue going to gigs at The Continental, even though at first I'm fearful I will see him there and be embarrassed, so soon after being mortifyingly rejected. He is never there.

Must have been at home having sensational sex with his wife.

I play Nina Simone singing 'Ne me quitte pas' on repeat. Two days after I start it up, a neighbour complains to me about 'people' who play the same damned song over and over again.

The poem I write about him leaving me is published in a prestigious literary magazine. Even this honour cannot assuage my misery.

∼

Dad's heart surgery is as successful as M— predicts. Weeks after it is over, on an afternoon I am visiting Dad at home, he looks up from his newspaper and says: 'Hey, San, whatever happened to that bloke you were seeing, the one who ripped open his shirt?'

'Finished, Dad. Not long after that afternoon.'

'Upset?'

'Yeah, fairly, at the time.'

'Still?'

'Only a bit now.'

'Hmm. What was his name? Never mind,' he says. 'His loss.' He gives the newspaper a shake and begins to turn the page. 'I know. M—, wasn't it? You'll be right.' He grins. 'Plenty more fish in the sea.'

There may well be, Dad, but there was only one M—.

The North Koreans
Come to Town

A two-man North Korean peace delegation arrives in town. They are here to attend a peace conference, a meeting of local peace activists and international guests organised by the Congress for International Cooperation and Disarmament.

The North Korean comrades bring with them a gift, the collected works of Kim Il Sung, inaugural president of the Democratic People's Republic of Korea, which they present to CICD's secretary, Dad. Physically, these volumes bear a striking resemblance to a collection by Joseph Stalin, which occupy a shelf and a half of a bookcase in Dad's study. The covers of these hardbound books – at least ten in the set (as there are in the Kim Il Sung collection) – are burgundy leather with gold type.

That evening, Dad phones. The North Korean comrades, one of them the vice-president of his nation, have a speech they wish to deliver the next day to ACTU president Bob Hawke. In the copy of the speech he's read, there's room for some improvement, Dad says – grammar, English usage, punctuation, that sort of thing. Would I tidy it up a bit, type it up for them?

At this time I am earning a living working from the front room of a single-fronted brick Victorian in North Carlton that I share with my friend Ginger. Here in this room, where I also sleep, I sit at a desk where, for an hourly fee, I type people's work: theses, stories, novels and so on. I have an electric typewriter, which, predating desktop computers as it does, is a very advanced specimen.

Dad tells me what time the next morning the delegates will be at my house. 'Shouldn't take you long,' he says.

~

The two men from North Korea arrive at 9.30. A black limo waits for them in the street. Each man is elegantly dressed in a dark suit (navy, as I recall), a gleaming white shirt and a medium-red tie; their highly polished shoes are black. One man has slicked back hair parted in the middle, the other a fringe that flops over his forehead, almost to his eyebrows. One carries a manila folder.

Each makes a shallow bow, and then, following the direction of my outstretched arm, enters my office space. The delegate who carries the folder hands it to me.

'Good morning,' I say, nodding only my head. What do the depths of nodding, of bowing, mean in Korean social etiquette? Is a head bow polite enough? Too familiar? I put out my hand to receive the folder. Another bow bestowed.

As neither has said a word, I presume they speak no English, so I indicate to them that I'm inviting them to sit down on the two chairs I have dragged into my office from the dining room. One of the men declines my offer, using sign language I take to mean 'Kind of you, but no thanks.' Instead, they stand, one on either side of me, just behind where I sit, close enough so they can clearly see what I'm doing as I type up their leader's words. Close enough to irritate me.

Can they read English? Speak it? Can they read body language?

Words of fellowship, the forging of relationship between our two great nations, peace, friendshio …

Oh, dear. A typo. I hold up my hand to indicate that I need to stop for a moment.

Alongside the typewriter sits a packet of Tipp-Ex, a correcting paper invented to eradicate typing errors without need of an eraser, which inevitably leaves a smudged mess of black ribbon ink on the page. Tipp-Ex comes in packets of ten small sheets.

I place the chalk-coated side of a Tipp-Ex sheet against my typo and bang out an 'o', and then type over the powdery error with a 'p'. Not an inky erasure smudge in sight. Magic. One of the men is gesticulating, asking me to show him what I just did, to show him what it is, this little piece of paper. He speaks excitedly to his comrade.

This time I use the Tipp-Ex to demonstrate: I deliberately make an error and fix it. Delighted, both men smile. It is obvious they have understood at once Tipp-Ex's magical quality.

'Please, what name is this?' Ah ha, some English. Comrade One takes a notepad from the inside pocket of his jacket, opens it to a blank page and prepares to write there with a fountain pen.

I show him the packet. He and his colleague nod enthusiastically, acknowledging what they have witnessed, the significance of the little packet. By the time Comrade One begins to write, I am also smiling. I reach into the desk drawer and retrieve an unopened Tipp-Ex packet. 'Here,' I say, 'have this one. Take it home.' I thrust it in his direction;

he raises his eyebrows and puts his hand on his chest. 'For me?' his gesture and eyebrows say.

'Yes, for you,' I nod.

He takes the Tipp-Ex, expresses his gratitude with a bow and secures the packet into the inside pocket of his suit jacket. The men are smiling, talking excitedly. My grin grows broader. P'yŏngyang typists, look out. Your working lives are about to change.

～

Dad says the speech went well, though it was way too long. I wasn't all that interested really. But I do like to think that in some small way I am responsible for improving the working lives of the women in the North Korean typing pools because I made a typing error on a day when two men from their country happened into my North Carlton house to have a speech typed up before they delivered it to their great peace-loving friends, the working women and men of Australia, via their representative Robert J Hawke.

Doves and Roses

It's nearly his birthday. What will I buy him? Ah, yes.

Since his retirement from business and, for all intents and purposes, from his lifelong political activism, he has taken up several … can I call them hobbies? Activities might be more precise. One is to prune the roses in the garden of the unit he and Mum now live in. In the big old house on the Alma Road hill, the garden path from the front gate to the front door was lined with roses, about twenty standards in all; he never paid them one skerrick of attention. Too busy with the business of his life. Now, ensconced in Elsternwick, with time on his hands, he has begun to prune.

Sometimes his rose pruning appears to be more an act of castration, or some other mutilation of someone lurking in his head – whoever raises his ire in this moment of pruning. A political enemy most likely, though possibly his mother, his brother … someone he's dredged up from his near or distant past. A harmless enough way to manifest his anger. Perhaps. Not that he would ever – he would never – understand pruning that way.

I've watched him prune a few times now. It is not uncommon to observe his pruning come to a point where it takes on a sense of 'Fuck. You.' about it.

~

In the garden beds of the unit Mum and Dad move to, six or seven standard roses have been planted. All are highly scented, all a little blousy, all loved by both parents, most of them bought by me – though not the Iceberg, a botanical cliché on which I would not spend so much as a penny. Apart from the Peace, a Just Joey and the Iceberg, I no longer remember their names, only the look and the fragrance of them.

After Mum dies and before the house goes on the market, Sister Two, Sister Three and I divvy up the plants from the garden beds and some of those in pots that stand on the bluestone back porch. My bounty is some mauve bearded iris, a crepe myrtle and a scrappy looking rose in a pot – dark red and highly scented when it bothers to bloom.

Dark red roses are not among my favourites, and this variety rarely displays itself in any way that might make it more appealing. The crepe myrtle doesn't appeal to me either, but I take it to give to my friend Marthe, just as I take the potted scraggly rose because I know Meri will to try to nurse it to health and enjoy it if it comes good.

~

One day, about three years after Mum dies, I visit Meri. We repair to the back porch to have a natter while we drink tea and smoke cigarettes. As we step out of the lounge room, I see a beautiful dark red rose, an old-fashioned single, growing in a pot on the porch. I put my nose to it, smell its scent and decide I must have one just like it. 'I don't usually like this colour, but this is a beautiful rose, Meri,' I exclaim. 'What kind is it?'

'I don't know,' she replies, amused. 'It's the one you gave me after your mother died.'

A twinge of regret ripples through me. I hope my friend isn't aware of it.

~

So, it's almost his birthday, New Year's Eve. After pondering the usual standbys for a while – chocolates? liquorice allsorts? a Peking duck? – a more creative idea comes to mind: I will buy him a Peace rose. Pale lemon petals with a pink blush along their edges. Blousy and fluffy when in full bloom. Sweetly scented. I feel sure he'll like it.

I buy the rose.

He likes it.

He thanks me, warmly, smiles when he reads the tag and says he will plant it tomorrow.

He hugs me, holds my head in his large, slender hands and plants a kiss on the top of my head.

~

As do the other roses, the Peace flourishes. Over the remaining years of Dad's life, the Peace grows to a respectable height, produces glossy leaves (no black spot) and prolific blooms. At one point I suggest he plant some chives alongside to keep away the aphids. He looks sceptical, so I explain. 'Companion planting, it's called.' To my surprise, he follows my advice. The Peace is never blighted.

At least once a week, when I'm visiting, he or Mum say, 'Look, Sandy. Look at how beautiful your rose is.'

~

The following year, a few weeks before Dad's birthday, I happen to be at a nursery in East Brunswick looking for a particular plant, its name long since forgotten. After fruitless searches elsewhere, someone tells me this nursery has a stock of them.

About to leave with my plant, I stand for a moment to gaze at the nursery's large collection of brightly coloured garden gnomes, glazed frogs of all sizes and alarming eyes and colours, clay birds and birdbaths, and all the other kitsch garden ornaments assembled there. The ugliness of them makes me smile. Just as I'm about to walk on, my eyes land on one of the birds. A white dove. A peace dove. A Picasso-like peace dove.

The dove could not have been whiter. All its features – beak, eyes, wings, feathers – are clearly defined; its tail is fanned out in grand display. It rests in a nesting position. This bird is an object of beauty in a field of tackiness.

'Happy birthday, Dad.'

Once again the smile of recognition, the hug, the kiss on the top of the head.

'Let's put it on the porch so it sits under the Peace,' he says.

Gently, he places the bird on a bluestone block nearest the Peace, there to rest in all its albino glory.

Two years in a row I please him with presents that are not a book, not liquorice allsorts, not a box of expensive fruit jellies, not even a crispy-skinned Peking duck from Victoria Street. None of the fallback presents.

~

Over the years the gleaming white dove turns a paler shade of grey. Dark green moss begins to bloom in the grooves of its wings and tail feathers. No one ever cleans the dove. Which is alright, because somehow, the moss looks as if it is meant to be there. In fact, it could be said that the dove wears its moss well.

~

About three years after Dad dies, someone knocks a garden chair into the dove and clips off most of its tail. That 'someone' is me. When I stand up to go inside to top up Mum's teacup, I whack the dove with the leg of my chair. I am mortified. More so when Mum, to my astonishment, bursts into racking sobs. Mum has rarely cried since Dad died, a fact she often remarks upon. It puzzles her: 'I still haven't cried, you know.' Today, she cannot stop.

'Oh, oh,' she wails, 'you broke his dove.'

Another occasion, another whack, which this time divests the dove of its beak. *Crack.*

There follows a stand-still moment, breathless, a gasping without sound, the widening of eyes, and then Mum and I looked directly at each other and start laughing. We laugh until tears run down our cheeks.

Whacking one of Dad's favourite presents? Wrecking the symbol of peace? And what of our laughter? Make of these what you will.

Maimed though it is, Mum refuses to throw away the dove. It isn't until after she dies, when my sisters and I are clearing out the house, that it is tossed onto the big skip we are sharing with the next door neighbours, who hire the skip for the building rubbish accumulated from their renovation. There the dove lies, on top of the mound of building detritus: wounded, battered, half-crushed. The sight of it breaks my heart; it makes me cry.

None of the sisters claimed the Peace from the garden, so there it remained with the other roses, in the garden of what had once been our parents' home.

～

About a year after the house is sold, I return there to ask the new owners if I may dig up a few iris rhizomes (a few more iris rhizomes). These plants, given to Mum by her sister-in-law, our Auntie Mim, come from Mim's mother Zoe's garden. Zoe inherits the irises when she and her husband Walter move into their house on the Caulfield side of Orrong Road, where Zoe lives until her late nineties. Mum has some of the rhizomes for at least thirty years, so by my reckoning these iris rhizomes must be at least one hundred years old. At least.

～

These days a young Orthodox Jewish couple, newly arrived from Israel with their first baby, live in what was our house. They answer the door together, the baby in his father's arms. Tall and lean, the young man wears the traditional at-home clothing of an Orthodox

Jew: a brilliantly white shirt and dark trousers, and a yarmulke; from beneath his shirt dangle the fringes of his *tallit*, his prayer shawl. His wife, a mere girl, is wearing a *shetl*, the wig worn by Orthodox women, possibly donned when I knock on the door, as she is not obliged to wear it indoors when she is alone with her husband.

We introduce ourselves. The husband is Yotam, his wife, Leah, the infant, Ari.

After I explain that this had been my parents' home and the purpose of my visit, Yotam and Leah warmly welcome me inside. 'Take whatever you need,' Yotam says.

Indoors, the rooms are sparse but at the same time chaotic. There is little in the way of furniture, no paintings, no ornaments. On the floor in what was once Mum and Dad's well-furnished lounge room, is a baby blanket, a few toys, a half empty packet of disposable nappies and an armchair, which seems to double as a changing table. Our heavy timber dining table and chairs have been replaced with a card table, on which is piled a truckload of takeaway food containers (most likely from local kosher shops and cafes); two foldaway chairs face each other across the table. The kitchen is a mess of stacked dishes and saucepans waiting to be washed, and still more takeaway containers.

'Come,' says Yotam. 'Come through. Here, the garden.' He extends his arm as if ushering someone who has never before seen their way from the lounge room to the garden.

He opens the colonial-style sliding door to the bluestone patio. Even before I step out onto the porch, I feel dismayed. It is obvious the judiciously installed sprinkler hoses have meant nothing. Almost everything in the garden is dead: the grass, once a shimmering green, is brown, riddled with weeds and dents because … who knows what caused the dents? The daphne near the back door, the scent of which used to waft into the dining room, stands now in bone-dry soil; a few dried brown leaves dangle from its otherwise bare branches. Plants in pots left behind, unwanted by any sister, have suffered much the same fate as the daphne. And the lemon tree in the middle of the lawn, once fecund, thriving after being rescued a few years earlier from some lemon pox or another? Dead.

The roses? I sigh. Moribund. The Icebergs? Dead. The Peace? Dead. Every last one of them, dead dead dead. At first I'm glad Dad and Mum aren't here to see the garden's demise, but soon realise that, of course, if they were here, there wouldn't be any demise to see.

Is this couple, I wonder, unconsciously trying to re-create the desert of their homeland?

They are so young, this Yotam, this Leah, standing there with their firstborn. They smile happily. Most likely they are not yet twenty. So many more children yet to come. Each tells me how happy they are to be in Australia, close to family who paved their way. When one speaks, the other nods in enthusiastic agreement.

All this happiness makes me determined to hold the line. I will not let them see how upset I am.

From my backpack I retrieve my trowel, squat in front of the iris bed and begin to dig. As I dig, I chew the inside of my cheek. Do not cry. Do *not* cry. I don't cry.

The rhizomes lift readily from the soil, ashen grey now, and powdery. After shaking loose any clinging soil that remains, I place the plants in a plastic bag, also retrieved from my backpack. Then, I stand up and prepare to leave.

Leah offers me tea. Not this time, I say, smiling, knowing there will be no next time.

Although the round of farewells is friendly enough, it's clear that Yotam and Leah's hearts are no longer in it; their attention has already turned back to their baby.

⁓

'Sandra!' Tova, the neighbour in Unit 1, is at the letterbox. I hear her delicious Israeli accent, her warm voice. 'Shalom, Sandra. What for you are here, dear girl? *Bist* OK?'

'Shalom, Tova. Yes, thanks, I'm OK. *Bist du?*'

Accented though it is, Tova's English is excellent. Sometimes she talks to me in Yiddish because she knows I understand a bit, speak a bit, that I enjoy learning more from her. She also knows that in the years before Mum dies, I asked Mum to *redst mit mir a bisl Yiddish*, to speak a bit of Yiddish with me, so I can learn yet more.

Tova knows that if I'm not sure or don't know what she's saying, I will ask.

'*Vos host ir dort?*' she asks, pointing to the plastic bag.

'Irises.'

'Come,' she says, looking at me more closely, then indicates in the direction of the front door with her head: 'Come. We'll have tea.' Not too long after her journey from Israel lands her in Melbourne, Tova learns the Australian cultural practice of the cup of tea as cure-all.

Almost seventy, Tova is a handsome, lively woman, with curly blonde hair and a sharp mind. Her front door is always open to me.

Before I go up the two steps to her porch, I pause for a moment and sniff the air.

'*Akh*,' says Tova. 'Always you loved dem feijoas. After, we'll get for you some to take home.' The tree, covered with fruit that none of the three unit owners has ever liked, is right outside her bedroom window. I set down the bag of rhizomes on Tova's porch.

'*Nu?*' she says once she's poured the tea.

I explain what I'm doing here that afternoon.

Tova is quiet for a moment. Then, with a perspicacity I have never given her credit for, she leans across the table and pats me on the cheek. 'Sendruh,' she says, pronouncing my name with a rolled 'r', 'I miss them too.' She lifts my hand from the table and holds it.

We smile sad little smiles at each other. Then Tova suddenly starts laughing. 'Oy oy oy,' she says as she laughs delightedly. She holds the hand that isn't holding mine against her chest, as if she's afraid her heart is going to pop.

'*Vos iz?*' I say. 'What?'

Tova catches her breath. 'She told me, you know, your mother,' Tova says. The skin around her eyes is crinkled in amusement; her eyes glint with merriment. In response to my questioning gaze, she says, 'How you smashed his peace dove.' She begins to laugh again. 'Twice.' Now her laughter becomes unrestrained.

Dismayed, I stare at her. 'She told you that?'

'She told me. *Far vos nischt?* Why not?'

At first I'm annoyed that Mum has gossiped about me wrecking the bird. Then, for the second time when contemplating the two whacks to the peace dove, and infected by Tova's laughter, I begin to laugh with her.

Me and Tova, we laugh as if we'll never stop. She squeezes my hand and stands up. 'More tea?'

Before I have a chance to answer – she has already begun to prepare us each a second cup – she turns, caddy in hand, and says: 'They both loved you, you know that, *yo?*' Then she sighs. 'I miss them, *du vayst?*'

'Yes, Tova.' I sigh as well. 'I know. I miss them too.'

'*Kumst mit mir*,' she says. 'I want to show you something.'

She leads me to the back door, the same colonial-style sliding door as Mum and Dad's, in which each glass square is framed by polished teak. '*Gibst a kuk*. Look,' she says.

There, nesting on a table on her bluestone porch, is a clay bird. It's not quite a dove, not really any discernible breed, but it is a bird. And it is white.

'I always liked that bird you bought for him,' Tova says. 'This one, I find it in that nursery on the corner of Kooyong and Glenhuntly. You know which one?'

I do know which one, though I never shop there.

'When I'm buying for the garden some punnets, I seen this bird.' She gestures towards it with her chin. 'It reminded me of your parents, so I bought it. So far, none from my kids broke none of it.' We stand for a minute or two, gazing at the bird. Then she takes my hand, gives a gentle tug and smiles. 'Come,' she says, 'let's pick for you some from dem feijoas.'

A Keffiyeh and Four Yarmulkes

On his travels in the Middle East, Dad receives a keffiyeh – the scarf worn by many Palestinians, particularly men – from Palestine Liberation Organization leader Yassar Arafat. Left-wing legend has it that Arafat drapes the folds of his keffiyeh from his head down to his shoulder in such a way that it resembles the shape of the land of Palestine.

Dad's keffiyeh is dense black thread on white cotton fabric. He gives it to me, but I prefer the one I already have (where did I buy it?), which is also black and white, but the pattern is less dense, the scarf less heavy. My daughter likes the Arafat keffiyeh, so I give it to her.

There is also a collection of yarmulkes, bought on his travels in various parts of the world. After he dies, I select the four I most like and take them home. When my grandchildren come with me to Passover at Cousin Annie's, each wears one of the yarmulkes: my granddaughter chooses the red velvet with a circle of fine gold embroidery thread around its circumference, 1 or 2 centimetres from the rim, my grandson, one of the black silver-embroidered pentangle-shaped yarmulkes from Tashkent, whose matching pair is worn by me.

The fourth yarmulke, a plain black silk that Dad buys in Paris, I plonk on the crown of a papier-mâché Chinese head that sits on a small Chinese inlaid cupboard in my lounge room. It disappears when I move house, most likely tossed out with all the rumpled paper in one of the tea chests. Its loss is not particularly disappointing, as it is only the Chinese head that ever wears it; neither the grandchildren nor I ever take any particular fancy to it.

Later, when my grandchildren lose interest and stop coming to the Seder, I give the yarmulkes to Cousin Libby, who leads our Seder service every year. I am comforted in the knowledge that the yarmulkes have – as has the keffiyeh – gone to a good home.

The Slipper Walloping Story

He has a range of stories. Limited, but a range all the same. When we are children, even when we are teenagers, he drags them out every couple of years to recount to a dinner guest – someone visiting for a peace conference, perhaps – or again for his family. Again. Their composition rarely changes.

There is the one about dressing up in plumber's overalls and carrying a plumber's toolkit into Bonegilla migrant camp in northern Victoria, where many Croatian immigrants reside. He goes to ascertain whether members of the Ustaše, a Croatian fascist organisation, have been permitted to emigrate to Australia following the Second World War. It is, he says, an action he carries out on behalf of the Jewish Council to Combat Fascism and Anti-Semitism. What he sees when he enters the shower block are naked men who, when they raise their arms to wash, make visible the Gestapo's insignia – the double SS lightning bolts – tattooed in their armpits.

The information gleaned from this investigation leads to campaigns by the Council to have these men deported. Which never happens.

Then there is the story about being under fire in New Guinea during the war when a voice comes over a rise: 'Cuppa tea, mate?'

The voice belongs to a member of the Salvation Army. When the Salvos come to our door rattling the tin during its annual collection drive, Dad gives the collectors a donation, a gift denied to every other tin rattler, whether they are at our front door or on the street. 'Government should be paying for this,' he says to those others, all huff and puff as he politely but firmly turns them away, often after delivering a lecture about how the rattler should proceed politically in order to obtain what their organisation needs.

Did he really venture to Bonegilla disguised as a plumber's mate, there to act out his role in the shower block? Was he in New Guinea? What is Samuel Mark Goldbloom, 46 Australian Infantry Battalion / 1 Engineering School, RAAF, doing under fire in New Guinea? What is he doing on the low side of a hill when the Salvos come over the top offering cups of tea? Did the Salvos come over the hilltops with cups of tea in New Guinea? Anywhere?

Several years after he dies, I ask Mum. She says what she says about several of the matters of his life: 'Bullshit story. He was never there.'

'Where was he then?' I ask, flabbergasted. Being long since dead, how could he ever refute her rebuttal? What's more, given this is one of the tales he tells unswervingly about his war service, why would he tell it any differently were he still alive?

'We can talk about this some other time,' she responds. 'I'm tired now. Have to go to bed,' or 'Have to go. There's something on the stove.'

After several such enquiries, Mum tires of me and refuses to ever speak of the story again.

Nor will she ever corroborate his tale about answering an advertisement in the military *Gazette* calling for personnel to learn Japanese.

He and one hundred and ninety-nine others apply. Samuel Mark Goldbloom, airforce aeronautical engineer, who can barely speak a word of Yiddish or any language other than English, is one of the chosen applicants – 10 per cent – who will be taught Japanese in order to act for the Australian and American military as an interpreter of Japanese prisoners of war. Those selected are to take their classes at the University of Melbourne.

Apart from mention of Queensland, one of the states where, he says, interrogations of the interned Japanese take place, no matter how many times he tells this story, there is a dearth of specifics about what exactly this work is, how long he does it for, in what circumstances it is done; there is never any description, physical or personal, of what the prisoners whose words he interprets are like.

Knowing Dad is hopeless at languages this story bothers me quite a bit. From the mid 1950s onwards, once his annual overseas travels to attend international peace conferences begin, he learns to say thank you and please in many languages; for comrade he uses the Russian, *tovarishch*. The few other words he speaks in other languages, most of them European, are the word for peace, some words for food (he particularly enjoys using *ananas*, the word for pineapple in France, Spain and Portugal) and drink, and questions about how to get to a bus or a train, to a toilet, or 'Where can I buy …?', all spoken with an appalling accent. Even in Yiddish his accent is not great. Yet if language can be understood as music – the rhythm, the sound, the cadence of it, – to me his Japanese seems perfect: emphases appear to be in the correct places, syllables are clipped where they are meant to be clipped, run together where they're meant to run together. He also seems to know the etiquette of bowing – shallow, medium, deep. Did he learn these in his travels in China or Japan?

~

Yet another story features Daisy Bates, the Irish anthropologist who, in the early twentieth century, lives among Aboriginal peoples. He recounts how he spots her from a train window somewhere on the Nullarbor Plain when, as a boy, he travels from Perth with his family to settle in Melbourne. Though, he concedes, it isn't until many years later – decades later – that he realises who the woman must have been.

~

It's the story about being given a thrashing by his father that most often makes me laugh, makes me like the grandfather I never met. It's not until late in my life that new thoughts, new ideas about this story surface and drive away the laughter.

Here it comes – again. He's settling in to tell the slipper walloping story. It's the story in which his mother tells him he's going to cop it when his father comes home, which is any minute now. 'Your father is going to give you a good hiding,' she says, for whatever the misdemeanour he committed this time.

Alexander Goldbloom comes home from his work as a bookbinder – *ayn bukhbinder*. His wife Frances, a fashion buyer for Georges department store, reports their younger son's misbehaviour. 'Alex,' Frances says, 'Sam has been a very naughty boy. Take him upstairs and give him a good hiding.'

'What has he done this time?' Alexander enquires.

Frances describes their son's misdemeanour.

'Very well,' Alexander says to his wife. He turns to his son. 'Samuel, follow me.'

As Dad begins to move this account up a gear, a smile begins to tweak the corners of his mouth.

'We go upstairs,' Dad continues. 'My father takes off a slipper and says, "You know what to do, Sam. Ready?"'

'I sit on the end of the bed and watch as the slipper comes flying through the air. The moment the slipper hits the pillow' – now Dad's smile is broad – 'I howl: Yeeoooowww.' To give the story greater effect, each time he says 'hits the pillow', he has, in recent years, taken to slapping his hand on whatever surface is available to him: table, chair, thigh.

Slap. 'Yeeoooowww.' *Slap.* 'Yeeoooowww.' And so on, until it has been deemed that enough punishment has been meted out, though whether in fact or only in his story is indeterminable. Each time Grandfather Alexander is done with the slipper slapping game, he says in a voice loud enough to be heard downstairs: 'Now don't let me hear of you doing that ever again.'

'No, Father.'

Father and son grin at each other, wait a few minutes, and then go downstairs together where they seat themselves at their respective places at the dinner table. Occasionally, this story is given an additional flourish – a coda, if you will: the boy Samuel, when he arrives in the dining room, rubs his backside and whimpers softly. His eyes are red around the rims, not from weeping (there was never any weeping, he says) but from rubbing, to make it appear as if there has been.

This story usually brings a smile to the face of everyone listening, especially his immediate family. Dad laughs too, enough to bring tears to his eyes.

There are many times that I wish he had been so playful when he was punishing me for my misdemeanours. That's not the way it happened between us. The slipper – the belt, the ruler, his hand – always lands, stingingly harsh, on my flesh: buttocks, legs. On each occasion, my eyes are always red from tears; they are never red from rubbing.

～

The once every so often, never know when to expect it school bag raid is on. He comes to my room and demands to check what's in there, as if this time there might be a surprise. I know what he's looking for; he knows what he will find. And there it is. A red and gold packet of du Maurier cigarettes that I've nicked from one of the cartons my parents buy at the local garage when they fill up.

'How many times have I told you ...'

More times than either of us can count.

'I'll deal with you later,' he says.

True to his word, he deals. He comes again to my room, looks to see what's available. His eyes land on my wooden ruler. 'You know what to do. Turn around.'

Whack whack whack *on my backside. I don't want him to see me cry, but the whacking is painful; I can't help myself. I cry and cry. My eyes turn red.*

What I have never been sure about is whether I'm being punished for smoking or for stealing their cigarettes.

～

Over two generations, the slipper walloping story maintains its currency. It is a mirthful account of a kindly father who loves his son and a mean-arsed mother, our Nanny, disliked by everyone in our family except me. During school holidays I stay with her, in her apartment in the back of her Warburton haberdashery shop. Nanny allows me one of the pleasures I'm denied at home: to read *Phantom* comics. My affection is a cheap buy.

～

Cruelty begets cruelty. Abuse begets abuse. This is what I learn.

As the many years pass I come to understand more about abuse, about post-traumatic stress, about the long-term effects of war on combatants, about the long-term effects of brutalities experienced by children at the hands of their parents or siblings or fellow students, and later, by those adults on their own children, their partners. In more years still, I come to learn something of mid twentieth-century and early twenty-first century psychological theories of abuse – how the experience of abuse is carried, often as physical as well as emotional pain, as trauma, as addiction, for much, if not all, of one's life.

～

Trauma. In those days, there was little or no help available to deal with the trauma returned soldiers experienced. Little or no help to deal with trauma of any kind, including – indeed, especially – being walloped by a parent. Later, when therapies do become more available, psychotherapy has, like everything else, long since in our house been allotted its slot on the political spectrum: it is, Dad declares, 'a bourgeois self-indulgence'.

For years before I turn myself over to this bourgeois self-indulgence, I believe – am for many years entertained by – the slipper walloping

104

story. Many years. It is only after a protracted period of therapy that I begin to wonder about it. In time, after lengthy and serious consideration, I come to no longer believe this story at all. I come to think that Dad's father, the Alexander he so loved, was probably a brutal man. As with so much else, the truth of this will never be known because at the time it doesn't occur to me to question its veracity, and so I don't enquire further. Indeed, it would never have occurred to me to suggest that there might be something else to this anecdote.

Now? Now, as with so many other things, there's no one left to ask. Even if there were, experience teaches me there is no guarantee any information will be forthcoming.

Fantasia

It isn't until almost twenty years after he dies that I hear a different story, a story never before told, whose telling shocks and confuses me.

∼

Valda Goldbloom, Dad's sister-in-law, dies in 2018. At her funeral, the eulogist, Cousin Laura's close friend Christine, talks a little about Valda's husband, Braham.

In the mid to late 1940s, Christine recounts, once the war is over, Braham Goldbloom and his young brother Sam, both now in their twenties, go to Princes Pier in Port Melbourne to await the arrival of ships bearing Holocaust survivors, many of them war-ravaged Jews who arrive as refugees in Australia, in what they come to call the land of milk and honey, *die goldene land*. Many are the only members of their family who have not been murdered, who survived the forced marches and the camps, or who were not killed by disease, starvation, torture, all the privations and cruelties meted out to them.

Once the ships dock and people pour down the gangplank, safe and secure on Australian soil ('on terra firma', Dad would say) where they will be resettled, Braham and Sam look for Jews among the new arrivals. Jewish Welfare will help these refugees to find homes, work, relatives, though some relatives are already there, waiting on the dock. Dad and Braham walk up and down the queues of new arrivals calling out: 'Any Jews here? Any Jews?'

The brothers put the Jewish refugees who don't have family in Melbourne in touch with appropriate welfare organisations that will help them obtain support from members of Melbourne's Jewish community: homes, even if temporary, are found, as is work.

~

This story moves me. Yet even more than it moves me, it unsettles me. Here is a good story previously untold. Why have I never heard it? Do the sisters know it? It is a recounting of a kind and compassionate gesture, a mitzvah, good deeds performed as an acceptance of religious responsibility. It's not that this act of kindness is out of character: throughout his life, he performs many mitzvahs, even though from the time not long after his bar mitzvah he has been an atheist. Why is it, then, that of all the stories he tells, this has never been one of them, certainly not within my earshot?

I try to picture them, the two tall, dark, red-headed, freckled Goldbloom brothers, striding purposefully along the thick wooden planks of Princes Pier where ships of all kinds dock: passenger liners, cargo ships, troop carriers that return to port with numbers greatly diminished from those they carried off to foreign wars, tugboats and now ships carrying survivors of the camps, refugees from all over Europe. As they walk along the queues, the brothers cry out, seeking Jews among the passengers.

Imagining that is the easy part. The never having heard the story before, the why of that is what's so puzzling. Come morning, I will phone Cousin Laura to see what, if anything, she knows about this tale.

~

Conversation with Laura brings even greater surprise, further perplexity. My cousin tells me that the eulogist at her mother's funeral does not recount this story. Even if she had, she would *never* have said that the brothers called out 'Any Jews here.'

Thinking about the notion of the two young men – of anyone – walking along a queue of refugees crying out 'Any Jews here?' to people who have managed to survive the war, the Holocaust … the insensitivity of it is ludicrous. Of *course* it would never have occurred.

So what then? Are Dad and Braham members of a youth group, or some other activist organisation whose members greet passengers from these ships?

Digging often leads only to more questions, questions that can sometimes never be answered.

If not at my aunt's funeral, where, then, did I hear this story? Where else could I have been to hear someone talking about Dad and his brother? Their social circles were completely different.

Is Laura's memory as undependable as mine appears to be? Laura is adamant that the 'Any Jews here?' aspect of the tale is completely wrong. I am just as adamant: I heard it at the funeral, I'm sure of it. There is no other explanation.

Besides, Laura says, she has never told her friend about what Braham did on the Port Melbourne wharves. Yet I remain just as resolute that she must have, even if she didn't tell the 'Any Jews here' part, even if she spoke only of the siblings helping to bring the refugees to settlement in Melbourne.

We are silent for a minute or two while I think. Slowly, slowly …

'I am absolutely sure I learnt this at Valda's funeral.' Pause. 'Maybe' – a light of memory is flickering – 'maybe I spoke with someone after the service, you know, when everyone was mingling, having refreshments.' My brow is furrowed. I am deeply puzzled.

Laura chuckles. 'That's right. You did. It was me. *I* told you. You don't remember.' Pause. 'I told you about Braham, but not about Sam. I have no idea whether he was there, but I don't think so.'

Now I am struck dumb.

'There is no way that Christine would talk about Braham at Val's funeral,' Laura continues. 'Why would she? Besides, she could only get that information from me, and I have never given it to her.'

Am I still, at my advanced age, so eager to idealise him, to be besotted by him, by his good deeds – his mitzvahs real and imagined – that I have projected him into his brother's story? Into a fantasy of what I would like him to have done? Did the brothers go down to the dock together? Did Dad go on other occasions but without Braham?

My cousin and I are silent again, a little longer this time.

After a while (I am grateful she is patient, that she doesn't hang up), I tell Laura that I will see what I can learn from Jewish Welfare, if archives are kept, if there are records of who did what for postwar Jewish refugees.

Before we hang up, I tell my cousin that I will let her know what, if anything, I am able to ascertain. Deep in my heart, I know what I'm going to find. Nevertheless, I press on.

~

Even less than what I anticipate – hope for – is to be found. After several enquiries, my knowledge is no further advanced.

Polly, a friend active among Holocaust survivors, doesn't know for sure but says it's possible it could have occurred. I tell her that I wrote an email to Jewish Research Services, which has gone unanswered. Polly suggests I contact her friend Max, who is also engaged with the Jewish community. Max has not yet replied.

Uncertainty lingers. *Did he? Didn't he?* Other than Laura, there is, yet again, no one left to ask, no one from whom I might expect any enlightenment.

But wait, the phone's ringing. It's Max, who tells me that after he receives my email, he does a bit of a search on Trove. No luck yet, Max says, but he'll have a deeper look. Write to Jewish Care, he suggests.

Jewish Care's website has a form that must be filled in before the organisation will release any information. Privacy reasons, the website says.

I print out the form, fill it in, fold it, slide it into an envelope, post it and wait. It suffers the same fate – I suffer the same fate – as my email to Jewish Research Services: my request for information goes unanswered.

~

Weeks after that initial conversation with my cousin, I concede defeat. I accept that Uncle Braham is the brother who goes to Princes Pier to greet refugees but Sam does not go with him.

I have come to accept, with not much grace and with considerable disappointment, that I confected the whole story about Dad and this particular mitzvah because, as old as I am, as dead as he's been for these many years, I still want to bathe him in additional glory. In so doing, I have attempted to take over my cousin's memory. Oh, not intentionally, with no malicious intent to be sure, but to at least insert Dad – and my fantasy of him – into her story.

Out of nowhere, unbidden, I realise I'm thinking about Pete Seeger's song 'Where Have All the Flowers Gone?' It makes me wonder about myself: when will I ever learn?

The Cuban Missile Crisis

It is 1962. US warships make rapid progress towards Cuba, once the playground of America's rich and (in)famous. For the next thirteen days, the world teeters on the edge of nuclear annihilation. President Kennedy puffs out his chest and threatens dire consequences if the Soviet Union doesn't remove its missiles from the Caribbean island, located ninety miles from Florida. Premier Khrushchev puffs out his chest and says the missiles are not moving. Brinkmanship. The world holds its collective breath.

Dad and I stand next to each other at one end of the living room. Mum is seated on the edge of the couch. Could it really be that, here, in East St Kilda, on our black and white television set, we are watching the end of the world? People everywhere are skittish about the looming threat of nuclear war, a threat the world has lived with since 1945.

At first we stand with our hands by our sides, quietly watching the screen at the opposite end of the room. As the newsreader continues with his update, Dad grips my arm to give me a reassuring squeeze. 'Sandy,' he says, 'even if this is the end' – he squeezes a little tighter – 'at least we know we did what we could to prevent it happening.'

I turn my head a little to look away from him, away from the television screen. Fearful as I am, I don't want him to see the smirk on my face. Even though I've uncritically followed his path into the peace movement, into support for the Soviet Union, into membership of the Communist Party, even though I am only nineteen, I know that the slogan on a poster many young Leftists have on a wall of their house – most often the lavatory wall – is what we are really in for. The poster provides information on how to proceed in the event of a nuclear attack. The last two points read:

6 *Immediately upon seeing the brilliant flash of a nuclear blast, bend over and place your head firmly between your legs.*
7 *Then kiss your arse goodbye.*

⁓

The crisis passes. The world lets out a collective sigh of relief.

For some years to come, after the non-nuclear dust settles on this particular Cold War episode, I wonder how afraid he was, if he just said those words to calm me, to calm Mum. It is quite possible, too, that he said them to calm himself.

Moscow Nights – and Days

St Basil's Cathedral in Red Square towers above me. I gaze skywards at the shapes and colours of its onion domes. No photo I have ever seen – there have been many – does justice to the beauty of these architectural wonders.

Hundreds of people amble around the square. Citizens from all the Soviet republics and tourists from many countries, not least the United States and Western Europe, are wandering around the square. A long queue of hundreds more is lined up to visit the mausoleum that houses the embalmed body of the first premier of the Union of Soviet Socialist Republics, Vladimir Ilyich Ulyanov, known to the world as Lenin. Standing in line holds no appeal for me; nor does seeing inside the tomb.

As I pause, pondering what I might do next, a young man, who appears to be not much older than me, sidles up. 'Yoo khave bloo jins? I giff yoo tollars.'

No blue jeans, I tell him. Disbelieving, he stares at me: a Westerner, a young Westerner, who does not have blue jeans to sell him? At least one pair?

I suppose I could tell him that he has the wrong sister, that in our family it's Sister Two who wears the blue jeans, but what would he care about a jeans-owning sister who isn't here to sell to him, so he can onsell and make himself a few roubles?

After one more try – '*Pliss*, you sell to me bloo jins' – he leaves, disheartened by my sorry can't help you shrug.

～

At the time of my nineteenth birthday, I am part way through my first European trip – London, Paris, Rome, Athens. Dad arranges for me to travel east to join the Australian delegation to the World Peace Council's Congress for Peace and Disarmament conference, to be held in the Kremlin's Palace of Congresses. Mum is also travelling in Europe; she too will attend as a delegate. Or, I wonder, might the purpose of her presence be to keep a watchful eye on me?

～

Mum and I arrange to meet in Rome. Dad's artist friend Giuseppe Zigaina is our tour guide. He accompanies us on a week of sightseeing, gallery crawling, eating at trattorias by day, outdoors in piazzas by night. One night, at the Baths of Caracalla, we take in a performance of *Aida*, replete with camels, elephants and a cast of hundreds. Overhead, the sky is a clear navy blue; the sun has almost set. Seated in this ancient ruin, something momentarily distracts me. Looking up, I see a jet aircraft, lights on, gliding across the sky. The plane has reached so great a height that its engines are inaudible.

From Rome we take a train to Florence, where once again we trawl galleries, from one to another, one garden to another, one trattoria to another, one concert after another. Four days after we arrive, Mum and I board a flight to Moscow. We arrive at Sheremetyevo Airport at midnight, where we are met by banished Australian journalist Wilfred Burchett, the first Western journalist to report on the devastation of Hiroshima. Burchett greets us warmly. 'How was your flight, Rosa? Hello, Sandra. How's Sam? Have you eaten?'

Burchett, who lives in Moscow with his Romanian wife, Vessa, drives us to the Hotel Ukraina, a grandiose confection in the Stalin-approved architectural style known derisively, if appropriately, as 'wedding cake'. Here we will stay for the next week.

Before we have a chance to go to our rooms to offload our suitcases, Burchett steers us into the hotel's restaurant, orders a meal for us in Russian and begins to chat.

Formally dressed waiters deliver us cabbage soup with sausage and caraway seeds, black bread, large red caviar, vodka. Burchett remarks on the vodka's excellence. Mum murmurs her agreement, but me, I don't know anything about that. By two o'clock everyone is exhausted. Mum and I find our rooms with the help of the Moscow equivalent of a bellhop, who loads our luggage onto a gleaming brass trolley and ushers us into the lift.

On our floor, a babushka is sitting on a low stool at the end of the hall, knitting, despite the hour. The babushka's hair is covered with a patterned three-cornered peasant scarf tied at the back of her head. She, or a replica of her, is seated at the end of the hall every day and every night of our stay. Just before he leaves us, the bellhop tells us in broken English that we are honoured guests, so if there's anything we need, just ask the babushka; she will be sure to get it for us.

Spasibo bolshoye, bellhop.
Pazhalusta, damy.
G'night, Mum.
Goodnight, Sandy.

Years later, while I wait my turn at a Melbourne doctor's surgery, I read in *Time* magazine that the babushkas at the end of the hallway on every floor in every hotel across the Soviet Union are, according to the author of the article, spies for the KGB, who keep an eye on all international guests, no matter what they are doing in the USSR, as well as on guests from the other republics in order to report their comings and goings to their masters. Is it true?

～

Seven short months have passed since Castro makes it official: he declares Cuba a revolutionary communist state. A mere four months have passed since the Algerians, after one hundred and thirty years of French colonial rule and seven years of war against the colonisers, declare their independence from France. Both delegations are warmly welcomed by multitudes of people from around the world, who pack the Kremlin's Palace of Congresses auditorium. Cuban delegates, arms laden, walk in a line up to the long presidium table, where they present the conference with hundreds of books, the size of large scrapbooks, filled with the simple writings and signatures of newly literate Cubans, a gesture that brings the house down. In fact, it could be said that in that moment the Kremlin rocked.

Theatrically, the Algerian delegation, members of the National Liberation Front, all wearing national attire, enter the auditorium to wild applause, to whistling and cheering.

Why isn't he here, Dad? His absence is unusual. Why am I here? Has he arranged for my participation as part of my ongoing political education? Why Mum, who, I feel sure, doesn't care one jot about being a delegate to a peace conference?

I never learn the answer to these questions, nor do I seek them out. At that time, there is no reason to seek them out. What I do know is that I am thrilled to be here, to hear the babble of so many languages, to see delegates in the national dress of the countries they represent, to see people from places I've read and heard about for so much of my life. To meet a man from Iceland.

'Why are you smiling?' His English is perfect.

'I'm thinking that you come from one end of the earth, I from the other. To me, that's something to smile about.'

'Ah, yes, it is,' he says, and grins.

It is all thrilling. I am thrilled. There are lectures to go to, activities to plan, meetings around issues delegates will bring to their peace groups, antiracism groups, others, once they get back home. Day and night there is music and theatre, there is dancing, there are sights to see, people to meet. There are no questions I need answered. Not then. Nor will there be for some time to come.

～

We Australians join a group of delegates from other nations to spend an evening at the Bolshoi Theatre – *Swan Lake*, as I recall. It is a grand night out in a grand old theatre that lives up to its legendary status. In between conference sessions, sometimes during, an Italian journalist and I go to galleries or for walks in parks and around Red Square. I ride the subway, get off at one station after another to gawp at the beauty of the architecture and sculpture, the exquisite floors, the hideously ornate chandeliers. *Chandeliers?* Yes, hanging from the roofs of many Moscow subway stations. GUM, the largest department store in Moscow – in the entire Soviet Union – is located on the northeast side of Red Square. GUM's interior architecture and design are magnificent, as is the building's exterior. Shortages, though, in several departments, mean many of its shelves are almost almost bare.

~

Khrushchev addresses the conference on its last day. There will be no shoe banging on the podium here. Why would there be? The assembled are, to greater or lesser extent, in agreement with what he has to say. For the first hour of his speech I sit with my headphones on, intently, dutifully listening to the translation of his address. Khrushchev rails against US imperialism, against all imperialism, against that war-mongering nation the United States of America, the threat the United States and its allies pose to the peace-loving Soviet Union. After the first hour I tire of him, of all the wisdoms and accusations I've heard myriad times. It's not that I disagree with what he has to say. After all, I've been raised right, haven't I? But an hour is more than enough. I nod off, to be woken by another of the Australian delegates.

'Wakey wakey, Sandra. Time to go.'

Khrushchev has addressed the conference for two and a half hours.

~

From Moscow, delegates from many parts of Europe, Africa, Asia, the United States and some of us from Australia travel on the famed

Krasnaya Strela – Red Arrow – the luxurious Moscow to Leningrad sleeper train. At the end of each carriage is a samovar where people gather to talk, sing, laugh, discuss, bumbling along in fragments of each other's languages, though many have at least fluent English or French. We help ourselves to tea. Some comrades have vodka or whiskey, which they pour shots of into their tea glasses. Everyone smokes cigarettes.

Travelling in the midnight sun latitude, we pass through superb silver birch forests. At around two or three o'clock, as the sun begins to set – it is a stunning sunset – people peel off to go to their bunks. In another hour or two, the sun will rise again.

Early in the morning, we arrive in Leningrad.

~

By the time I write this story, Leningrad has long since been renamed St Petersburg, its pre-revolutionary name. I am unable to bring myself to call it that, not only because it is Leningrad when I meet it and what I grow up calling it, but also because to revert to St Petersburg, its name in tsarist times, feels retrograde.

Leningrad is a beautiful city of wide boulevards, parks and lakes. Every night in the many rotundas scattered throughout each park, bands play all manner of music, including some gentle jazz. Sixteen years after the end of the Second World War, the scarcity of men in the population remains plain to see. Hundreds of thousands of citizens died of starvation and from fighting to defend their city during the nine hundred day siege by the fascists. Thousands more, among the many who managed to flee ahead of the advancing German army, also perished. Everywhere we go women far outnumber men: on the streets, in shops and in the parks, where they stroll together arm in arm, dance or sing together to one or another of the bands. Of the men we see, many are walking wounded; some hold themselves up with crutches, others get around in wheelchairs, either by their own efforts or with the help of others. Those men who we see have haunted looks in their eyes, lost limbs, disfigured faces. Scenes as dreadful as they are poignant.

Many men are fall-down drunk, rowdy drunk.

Nights are balmy, so each night we have free, we go in multinational pairs, trios, quartets to a park, to stroll, to sit around and talk and to smoke papirosa, those Russian cigarettes made of half cardboard tube attached to a half-sized cigarette of rolled tobacco. We go to watch the passing parade, to dance, to listen to music. Dotted around the parks are icecream carts. People queue for a cone. Someone says, 'Russians sure do love their icecream.' In this, at least, they are no different than anyone else, anywhere.

~

At the Hermitage Museum Mum and I take our time to wander around. Awed, we go back more than once. There is so much art to see that I am overwhelmed. On every gallery wall are paintings by artists whose work I have only ever seen in books. Among the Hermitage's vast and splendid collection are many of the artists whose works I studied at school. We wander through, gaze and gawp at art in Leningrad as we did in Rome and Florence. Earlier, before Italy, in Paris, too, at Le Louvre.

On more than one occasion I gasp, enthralled by the wonder and beauty of the many familiar images. Not one colour plate in any book I have ever looked at, studied, learnt from, can compare.

~

Mum and I take photos of each other standing in the forecourt of the Winter Palace. I am wearing a sleeveless royal blue cotton frock covered with white polka dots the size of two-shilling pieces and white winklepicker flatties. Here, no one offers to buy my clothes or my shoes. We ask a passerby if he will take a photo of us. The passerby obliges.

Once our Leningrad holiday is over, Mum returns to Italy and I board a train to Helsinki, where I am to attend the Eighth World Festival of Youth and Students as a member of an Australian delegation. Some Americans I meet in Moscow, who also come to Leningrad, are going to Helsinki for the festival. We agree to travel together. A train will take us – take all the delegates leaving from Moscow, Leningrad and other points along the way – to the Helsinki station.

~

One Canadian winter Dad comes to visit. A week earlier I call my parents to tell them that Jack and I are separating, that I'm in love with another man and I'm going to run off with him.

Rani is one of the Americans I meet in Helsinki. An African American – 'Negro' in the 1960s – from New York, he is tall and lean; he is as smart as a whip and he makes me laugh. He tells me his name is a Hindi name. His mother, he says, had expected to give birth to a girl, but when she was delivered a son she kept the name after she learnt Rani is usable for a boy child as well.

Rani tells me his grandfather was a seafaring Australian Aboriginal, but in the two weeks we spend together I can never determine if he tells me this in order to ingratiate himself with me or if his tale is true, even when he insists, which he does a number of times, that it is. American chemist

Linus Pauling (a guess who's coming to dinner guest) is Rani's hero. He plans to emulate his hero and graduate as a biochemist.

Together we attend concerts, forums and seminars, meet friends in cafes and go to picnic in parks dense with silver birch. We wander the Helsinki streets and find quiet corners away from the international crowd to have sex.

Wildly, passionately, I am in love. Rani is the first of the great loves of my life.

'You are just like my dad,' I tell him, often.

I remember him chuckling, but little else by way of response.

On our return to our respective countries, we keep in touch for a while, but not for long. Later that same year, Jack and I marry and leave the next day for Toronto.

~

The train is decked out with bright red bunting, as are the stations we stop at along the way. Komsomol (Communist Youth League) members dressed in their traditional uniform of white shirt or blouse, navy pants or skirt, black shoes and a scarlet three-cornered scarf tied in front line the platforms, waving Soviet flags. They welcome us with robust renditions of 'The Internationale', cheering and calling out greetings. Once all the local delegates are on board, the Komsomol wave and sing us on our way.

Every station we stop at on the Soviet side of the border, the same.

~

Some time in the 1970s, I go with friends to the Rivoli Cinema to see Bernardo Bertolucci's Novecento. *A scene in which striking workers are*

123

brought from the fields by train to Communist Party polling booths elicits a memory.

From both sides of the slow-moving train, protruding at 45-degree angles, are poles bearing red flags that flap in the breeze. Matching red bunting bedecks the train, end to end. At the front of the steam engine, two flags point forward to a red future. Delighted by this familiar scene, I lean into my companion and whisper, 'I've been on that train.'

My friend shushes me and says to wait until after the film. Which I do, but waiting doesn't dampen my pleasure. What I understand, what is confirmed, in this cinema is that I am – have always been – part of a continuum of people from around the world who ride the red rail.

~

Filled with comradely fervour on my return to Australia, I join the St Kilda branch of the Communist Party. Six months later, my enthusiasm for branch membership wanes, so I allow my membership to lapse. It is not until 1972 that I rejoin, this time in the newly formed Carlton branch, whose membership is mostly young academics. I am elected to the state committee where, I soon realise, I am completely out of my depth among comrades with far greater political smarts than mine and who do not approve of our branch. This time I last for about two years.

~

Few of my friends show any curiosity about my travels to the Soviet Union, nor in my attendance at the Helsinki youth festival. Despite my eagerness to recount tales from the front, despite my breathless beginnings, I am cut off at the pass. Two or three friends or acquaintances show any interest. At two of the coffee lounges I frequent, some people greet me with raised clenched fists and derisive greetings: 'Comrade Sandra', 'Tovarishch Goldbloom', they say, and, snidely, 'How is life in the workers' paradise, comrade?'

For a time, I swallow my pride and press on, but in the end, embarrassed, hurt, I stop going to the old haunts. Stalwarts as well as new friends – people who don't mind my politics, others who agree with them, still others who don't agree with them but become friends all the same – suggest other places we can go for coffee, a meal, a conversation. I am grateful.

~

Decades later – three to be precise – I read a Martin Cruz Smith novel. Not *Gorky Park*, his most famous, but another, early one in which there is a character who has been to the Helsinki Youth Festival.

As it happens, Cruz Smith is a down the road neighbour of some friends of mine who live in the Pacific Northwest. This connection gives me, I feel, a leg in the door to write to him. There is an email address on his website.

Dear Martin Cruz Smith

We have mutual friends in your neighbours M— and W—.

I recently read your novel Red Square, *in which you mention the Helsinki Youth Festival. I thought I was the only person alive who would remember that event. How do you know about it? Were you there?*

Best wishes, Sandra Goldbloom Zurbo

Despite its brevity, despite being almost terse, his reply – 'That's for me to know' – nevertheless seems to have a knowing smile in it.

No further correspondence is entered into by either party.

Can You Keep a Secret?

After returning from Europe, I tell Mum that I have decided to join the Communist Party.

'Tell that bullshit to your father,' she hisses.

'Dad …'

He smiles when I tell him. 'Goodonya, Sandy.' Then, placing a forefinger against his lips, he whispers, 'Shhh, this is a secret. Can you keep a secret?'

We are standing in the lounge room, yet he looks over each shoulder as if there might be someone lurking, listening, someone who shouldn't hear his secret. 'I'm a member myself,' he says, his voice almost a whisper. 'That's our secret. You mustn't say anything to anyone.'

Can you keep a secret?
Tell me if you can.
You mustn't laugh, you mustn't cry
Just do the best you can.

Who could that lurking person be? Special Branch? ASIO, with its devices tapping our phone, possibly in other unsuspected places in our house?

We know our phone is bugged, that there are snitches in the organisations he belongs to and in the Youth Peace Group that I belong to, so why bother to whisper this secret as if I didn't already know it, at the very least hadn't already guessed? As if the security organisations didn't already know it?

But this is 1962, still the Cold War period, a time when some comrades continue to hide from Special Branch by using the false names they gave themselves in the 1950s when Menzies attempts to ban the Communist Party. Fearful of being raided, they hide their books by Left-wing authors, hide their copies of Marx and Lenin, hide the dusky-red covered Red Book Club books. They deny their membership of the Communist Party.

As later research into his and my ASIO files will prove, they are listening.

~

David, a friend and comrade, takes me to the home of Ralph and Dorothy Gibson, who, in the 1930s but independently of each other, become members of the Communist Party of Australia. When it comes to a lesson in how to thwart eavesdropping spook agencies, Dorothy and Ralph's method seems to me, for its day, to be particularly creative.

At the Gibson house, the phone is shrouded in two beautiful, double-knitted tea cosies that surely muffle the sound of any conversation – on the phone, around the table – from eavesdropping ears. Does Dorothy knit the cosies herself, I wonder, or does a sister comrade knit them for her?

~

Many people know of my father's Party membership. Many more carry a strong suspicion, despite his protestations to the contrary and his Labor Party membership; he is aware of that. What about Party members themselves? People active in the peace movement? Some – probably many – of them know too.

Most troublesome about being entrusted with his secret is how I should respond when people ask me about it, which happens often. How can I keep his secret, remain loyal, and not tell a lie? For a long time I remain *shtum*. When I first begin to answer I lie. 'No, he isn't,' I say, wracked with discomfort, blushing, shuffling from foot to foot – in my imagination if not in fact – before their sceptical or disbelieving gaze, their smirks.

Some time after being entrusted with – ensnared by – The Secret, I devise an answer that satisfies all my criteria. 'Isn't your Dad …?' I look the questioner in the eye and say: 'He's always said he's not,' which becomes my standard reply, because that at least is true. Sometimes I add a shrug, one of those I've got no idea shrugs that's accompanied by a downward turn of my closed lips. Whatever I say, whatever embellishments I perform, it is likely few people believe me, yet for whatever reason the response seems to mollify them; few press me further.

In certain quarters, particularly when I am at high school, fellow students filled with a certitude that requires no response insist: 'Your Dad's a stinking / filthy / rotten / Red / Jew' – pick an adjective or make for yourself a combination – 'commie. Why dontcha go back to Russia?'

Biff. Ouch.

～

He is twenty years dead before I feel comfortable enough to reply directly to people who remain curious, people who suspect they know: 'Probably,' I first come to say, and then, eventually, 'Yes, he was.' Each time, I feel my face burn with shame. *Rat*, I say to myself. *Snitch. Betrayer. You are a disloyal daughter.*

~

Tea cosies, cautions about what to say and what not to say on the telephone, these are one thing. Being followed is another.

Back home after my adventures in Moscow and Helsinki, Dad offers me a job as a sales rep. I agree to give it a go. Each day, when I come out of the drive with a selection of the small electrical appliances Mum and Dad sell to retail shops from their wholesale business run out of our garage, there he is, an Australian replica of a G-man, an FBI operative, possibly Special Branch's man, possibly ASIO's, the visible form of the unseen snoop who listens in on the telephone. Decked out in a suit – is it navy or grey? – discreet tie and black shoes, in a show of false respect to make sure I know he's there, he lifts his grey fedora a short way off his head. As he puts it back on, he says: 'Good morning, Sandra. Off to work, are we?'

Though I've never met this man, he knows who I am, just as I know who he is.

'Don't worry about him,' Dad says. 'Just go about your business. He's just trying to moz you.'

The government man follows me for part of the day; I go about my business. Each morning for most of a week the man is there, at the gate, politely greeting me as I leave for work. His presence doesn't moz me.

129

Will he report on me to his colleagues? To his boss? I suppose he will.

That spook, I bet he knows Dad's secret. What's more, I'm sure it is not a secret he has any trouble keeping.

Moratorium: a sliver

In the first of what will be the largest of the two Vietnam Moratorium Campaign demonstrations, after months of planning and political squabbling between groups about tactics and procedures – CICD, the Labor Party, Monash Labour Club, Students for a Democratic Society, Save Our Sons, trade unions, several denominations of church, the Worker–Student Alliance, the Communist Party of Australia, the Communist Party of Australia ML, Women's International League for Peace and Freedom, Pax Christi and others – the May 1970 moratorium finally takes place.

Thousands across the country participate. People of all stripes, yes, including conservatives and Liberal Party members who no longer approve of the war, walk side by side with unionists, students, housewives, church folk and those who never supported Australia's involvement, who are dubious about conscription. Office workers, tradies, seamen, wharfies and other workers walk off the job; many participate under their union banners. (Later that year, for the second Moratorium, the main slogan is STOP WORK TO STOP THE WAR. Bearing their union banners and other banners and flags decorated with this moratorium slogan, thousands of unionists walked off the job to join the march.) In cities, regional centres and small country towns, people gather to protest Australia's involvement, to protest against conscription, to protest the death of Australian soldiers and the slaughter of the Vietnamese people.

～

The morning of 8 May dawns bright and sunny; there is a light sea breeze. It's a perfect day for a demo. Dressed in socialist red – trousers and matching top – I take a tram to the city. Even though it is midmorning and rush-hour commuters are long since settled at their desks or behind shop counters, trams are packed as though it is peak hour. St Kilda Road is vibrant. There is a sense of movement different from the cars, buses and trams that usually ply their way along Melbourne's grand boulevard. A frisson charges the air. People walk in small groups, in pairs and alone; they ride bicycles and can be seen in large numbers on trams and buses as they head towards Treasury Gardens, the gathering place.

～

Colleagues, comrades, friends, they all laugh at him when he estimates that up to forty thousand people will take part in the Melbourne march.

'Sam,' they say with a smile, 'you're such a dreamer. Twenty. If we get twenty thousand it will be fantastic. It will be a good day.'

'No,' he retorts, 'more. You'll see.'

～

At the same time, in a suburb central to wherever they live, people in their hundreds are participating in radial marches that will converge at the Treasury Gardens. Along the routes, participants encourage onlookers to join them; many do. Upbeat, the marchers sing:

I'm gonna lay down my sword and shield
Down by the riverside
Down by the riverside …

People's clothes are dotted with protest buttons, especially but not only the moratorium's own, designed by my husband, Jack, as well as buttons bearing slogans of support for the National Liberation Front, for this cause and that. Many people carry flags and banners, including the red and blue yellow-starred flag of the National Liberation Front. Resolute, many of the marchers chant:

Ho, Ho, Ho Chi Minh
The NLF is going to win.

Perhaps he's right, I think, as I watch trams inch their way towards Princes Bridge. Usually, if there's a hold up in the city, trams retrace their route from south of the bridge and head back along St Kilda Road rather than continue up to the terminus at the north end of the city, but unable to move backwards or forwards, trams are banked up northbound on St Kilda Road and southbound on Swanston Street.

From all the compass points around the city marchers come.

There was movement at the station
For the word had passed around …

Somewhere on Bourke Street – about the corner of Exhibition near Thomas' Music – I see Dad as I make my way to the Treasury Gardens. 'Dad,' I call out. 'Dad,' louder over the hubbub.

He stops, turns to locate my voice, spots me (how can he not, me decked out in red?) and waves happily. 'See? What did I tell you, Sandy? Twenty thousand tops, they said. My arse.' Triumphant, he grins broadly, flings an arm around my shoulders, gives me a squeeze and says, 'Gotta go. They're waiting for me up there.' He strides off to join the other organisers and speakers, who are getting ready to address the crowd from a large stage.

〜

As ever, Dad's speech is rousing. Later, a friend suggests to me that he is a demagogue. Which of several possible meanings does my friend give to this term? Before I get the chance to ask him, he is gone.

Once done with the politics, Dad exercises one of his great skills: spruiking the cause in order to winkle donations out of people's pockets. It is, as always, a performance of theatrical proportions. Marshals and other volunteers bearing plastic buckets make their way through the throng to collect donations from participants, money that will further the work of the VMC. Thousands of dollars are raised, much of it in coin. When the buckets are returned to the Moratorium office, they are emptied into large plastic rubbish bins that are filled almost to overflowing.

Speeches over, donations collected, the massive crowd, a giant multicoloured slow-moving creature, begins to make its way out of the gardens and over to Bourke Street, where a sitdown will take place. Already an overflow of thousands, unable to fit into the packed gardens – not even to squeeze in – is amassed along Spring Street, all over the Parliament House steps and across the road.

〜

Several of the organisers make up the frontline of the demonstration. They march with arms linked: Dad, the Labor Party's Tom Uren, Jim Cairns and Clyde Holding, Save Our Sons convenor Jean McLean, Students for a Democratic Society activist Harry van Moorst, Electrical Trades Union secretary Ted Innes and others take up the lead of the Melbourne march of one hundred thousand people who walk – shuffle, more precisely; there are too many people to move much faster than a shuffle – from Treasury Gardens along Spring Street and into Bourke Street. There, protesters fill that wide street, east–west and north–south. They spill over into Swanston as far south as Flinders, and north to Lonsdale Street.

As a marshal I am equipped with a megaphone: 'Keep moving, people,' 'Move along, please,' and 'There are still people trying to come out of the gardens, so please move up.'

As well as Bourke Street being packed with demonstrators, its footpaths are also lined on both sides, with people watching, four, five, six deep. A few boo, most applaud, some hold up placards of support. One woman, bible held aloft, yells admonitions. Just outside Myer, another woman, also holding a bible to the heavens, shouts that Jesus will save us. Some shops have locked their doors against us, the invaders. Elsewhere along the street people hang out of office windows, and shop assistants stand in their doorways to watch, clearly amazed. And why wouldn't they be? We, the marchers, the marshals, the organisers, all of us are amazed. None of us expected it, not this scale; no one has seen anything like it in Melbourne before.

The sound equipment is inadequate for many to be able to hear Jim Cairns' speech, which he delivers from the back of a flatbed truck in the middle of the crowd. People sing antiwar songs, the Australian

Performing Group entertains the crowd with antiwar theatre, people talk among themselves about the turnout and what it means.

~

A concert of folk and rock'n'roll music is planned for the Sunday. Despite poor weather, it is agreed the concert will go ahead. The lineup includes progressive rock band Spectrum, singer–songwriters Ronnie Burns and Co Caine, blues artist Wendy Saddington, folk singers Glen Tomasetti and Margaret RoadKnight, and the Australian Performing Group. Four draft resisters – Tony Dalton, Paul Fox, Mark Taft and Tim Harding – burn their draft cards on stage.

Hell no, we won't go.
Hell no, we won't go.

It is, at that time, the largest concert ever held in Australia, and remains larger than any of the Sunbury rock concerts, the first of which will occur two years later. The Treasury Gardens concert is organised by the event's MC, Val Noone, at that time still a Jesuit priest, and me.

In Melbourne, the whole Moratorium weekend is one mighty successful political and musical gig. Although the demonstrations elsewhere in the nation are not as large as Melbourne's, each is huge and just as successful.

~

Despite the number of people who participate in the march and the broad spectrum of their political views, our efforts do not bring the war to an end.

Conscription ends soon after the Whitlam-led Labor Party wins the federal election. The final and complete withdrawal of Australian troops occurs later that year, 1972.

~

The day before the 1972 election, my partner, Chris, a draft resister who manages to evade authorities for a number of years by hiding in plain sight, is finally caught: two Special Branch heavies thump on our front door. Anticipating who's come knocking (no friends would knock so demandingly), Chris hides out in the back of the house. Scornful of my denials – 'Chris doesn't live here; he moved out months ago' – one of the disbelieving officers tosses the warrant through the opening in the door I'm closing on them. The paperwork lands on the hallway floor.

'It's inside the house,' one of the men shouts, 'so you're served.' Hastily, they leave.

The warrant for draft evasion advises Chris that he is to appear in court on a nominated date. What will be the outcome of tomorrow's election? Whitlam has promised to abolish conscription altogether and create an amnesty for resisters. Anxiously, glued to the television set together with friends the next night, we watch the election results come in, barely able to breathe.

Labor wins. Delirious uproar, cheering, relief. Chris is saved from staying on the run; he is also saved from appearing before a magistrate and the likelihood of a jail term.

~

While the war continues and spreads into Laos and Cambodia, smaller and ongoing demonstrations continue over the next three years.

The size of the Melbourne moratorium demonstration will not be eclipsed for another thirty-five years, when between 150,000 and 250,000 unionists and other citizens (the number depending on whose figures you choose to accept) demonstrate their opposition to John Howard's WorkSafe legislation.

Moratorium organisers and participants are proud to learn that, on 8 May 1970, on a per capita ratio, Australia has a larger number of protesters against the war than another other nation. We did well.

~

That moment when I see Dad in Bourke Street, I tell him before he heads off to the gardens that I'll see him at home – his – after the demo. But when I get there he hasn't arrived yet, so I sit with Mum for a while, recounting what went on, how it felt to be there, the numbers, the feeling among the crowd, the colour and spectacle of it. She watches some of it on the early news.

We talk for a while, but I'm weary now and want to go home, so I say goodbye, give her a hug and leave.

Later she tells me that Dad arrives only half an hour after I leave. For the next few hours, he can't stop talking, she says, that he flipped from one news service to another, even the tabloid channels. It isn't often she's ever seen him so happy.

Peep

Summer sun is melting the footpath.

Already, after only three months in Castlemaine, a once-was goldmining town in Central Victoria, I struggle with the relentless, searing heat of my first summer here. Already I miss the beach, the sea breeze.

One midweek morning I decide to slip on my backpack and head into town to the supermarket, an up hill, down dale walk of about one and a half kilometres. Another one and a half kilometres back again, this time with a laden backpack.

On my way home from shopping I become aware of an elderly woman walking towards me. Seeing her brings a smile to my face because she looks like Peppermint Patty grown old.

The woman's hair, grey and straight, falls to somewhere between her earlobes and her chin. It is parted on the left; the hair on the right side is held off her face with a bobby pin. Her linen clothes are practical: loose-fitting trousers and a white short-sleeved linen blouse, sensible walking shoes. Despite the practicality of her outfit, she looks stylish.

Even in the heat my walking pace is cracking; I can't help myself. The woman's is slow, almost but not quite a shuffle. Did she use a walking stick? I don't remember.

We pass each other without acknowledgement, but a few steps on, I realise that looking like an aged Charlie Brown cartoon character is not all that is familiar about this woman. I stop and turn. 'Peep?'

The woman also turns. 'Yes?' She shields her eyes from the sun. 'Do I know …?' She frowns, leans towards me a little. 'Sandra? Is that you?' Then, when she realises it is, she smiles and says, 'What are you doing here?'

It *is* her. Even if physically I don't recognise her at first, her voice, made husky from smoking cigarettes, is unmistakeable.

'Peep! How are you?'

My pleasure is unbounded, as, I believe, is hers. This woman has been in and out of my life since I was a teenager and I've always liked her. A lot. She is smart, straightforward, a lot of fun and when I was a child she never patronised me.

Peep's eyes flash bright with intelligence and laughter. Her grey hair was once ginger; her naturally pale face, once covered with ginger freckles, is wrinkled, though traces of the freckles remain.

Peep is a member of the Communist Party of Australia before its demise, and a peace activist for much of her adult life. For many years – on again, off again – she and Dad are lovers.

We exchange how are yous, but it is too hot to stay chatting on the street, so I give her my phone number and we agree she will call so we can make an arrangement to meet.

～

On the first occasion of what would have been Dad's birthday, New Year's Eve, Mum and I drive to the St Kilda Botanical Gardens where his ashes are scattered. It is a beautiful afternoon: unseasonably cool but sunny, bright; the sky is the clearest blue.

Each of us brings something to read – a book for Mum, a journal for me – though neither of us opens the pages. Mum also brings some fruit. We make ourselves comfortable, then I wait to follow her lead. If she wants to talk, we'll talk. If it's reading she prefers, we'll read.

'Nu, Sam,' she says the moment she settles herself onto the gazebo bench, 'are you up there shtupping that red-headed bitch?'

'Mum, cut it out!'

'Are you?'

'Cut it out, will you.'

'OK, OK. I've finished. Let's sit quietly now. Here, have some fruit.'

Forgoing the fruit, I light up a cigarette and inhale hard.

~

Peep and I meet at a cafe halfway between her house and mine. Over coffee and nothing to eat, we reminisce about our shared past (though not – yet – about Dad), about the politics of then and now, about life in Castlemaine, which she enjoys more than I do at that time, about art and books, about … *chit chat chit chat*. Nothing earth shattering, nothing too deep, simply an amiable conversation. I am happy to be in her company.

Barely noticed, two hours pass, at the end of which another arrangement to meet is made, same place. It's not that it's a great cafe, but it is convenient, and the garden out the back is a pleasant place to sit. Will either of us mention Dad next time?

~

We talk a little about him: his contribution to world peace, his tireless efforts to bring about nuclear disarmament. We also continue some of the same conversations we had at our first meeting: books, composers, political events, a bit about painting. The same all the same. Our conversation segues into gardening, a pleasure for both of us. We agree to swap this plant and that next time we meet.

But now, enough. It is time to take the bull by the horns.

'I owe you an apology, Peep,' I say.

Surprised, she replies, 'What? What for?'

'For what I said to you at Dad's memorial service.'

Peep is silent for a moment, then, 'Oh, that. That's alright.' Clearly she does not need to be reminded what it is I'm apologising for.

~

Peep walks towards where Mum and her three daughters sit. Her footsteps, along with the footsteps of the many gathered for the memorial in the South Melbourne Town Hall, tap loudly on the polished wood floor of the town hall's high-ceilinged function room. Peep offers her condolences to us all. Mum accepts them with cold politeness.

'Thank you, Peep.' Mum's iron gate is up. She does not put out her hand to shake Peep's. Peep can see there is no point in moving forward to hug her lover's wife or to shake her hand or … or anything really. She begins to drift away.

I stand and go after her. 'Peep.' We hug. Up close, she looks to have been crying. We talk for a few minutes; then, without any thought at all, with no consideration, I touch her on her forearm and say: 'You had an affair with him, didn't you?'

I want my remark to sound as if I understand the depth of her grief. Does it? Does it sound as if I'm acknowledging her pain? Am I smiling? I seem to remember smiling. Am I showing off about knowledge I think I have, even though it is only surmise?

Peep gasps, turns on her heel and, without a word, speeds away to the farthest corner of the town hall.

Left standing in the middle of the room, I greet and thank people coming into the hall: friends, family, colleagues, comrades, a doctor and some of the nurses who cared for him during his hospital admissions, who offer their condolences, kind words, words of admiration for Dad and how he lived his life. After each moves on, I forget who it was. Mortified by what I have just done to Peep, my responses are wooden, my smile stiff.

Fewer than five minutes pass before Peep comes back to me. Before she has a chance to speak, I apologise profusely. 'It's none of my business,' I say. 'I'm terribly sorry. Please forgive me.'

Peep starts to explain. Again I say it's none of my business, that she doesn't owe me any explanation. Again I apologise, tell her I'm ashamed I put her on the spot, that I shocked her, especially at his memorial.

'We did,' she says, 'but it was complicated. I cared about him a lot.' She pauses. 'How did you know?'

We hold hands.

I tell her I'd guessed, I suppose because of how he spoke about her, about what I observed when they were together, and that because I like her so much I didn't mind they'd been lovers. I did not say we knew there had been others. Did Peep know there had been others, or at least guess it?

'Things are about to start. I'd better get back to Mum.'

Peep gives my arm a squeeze. She kisses my cheek and says, 'Take care, Sandra.'

'You too, Peep.'

I return to my place next to Mum.

'What did she want? What were you talking about?'

'Nothing much. She just wanted to offer me her condolences and tell me how much she'll miss Dad.'

'I'll bet she will,' Mum snaps. 'Quiet now, things are getting started.'

After the memorial service, there will be an occasional phone call between me and Peep, or we might see each other at a function, but that is all for many years. I hear on the Left-wing grapevine that she has moved with her partner to Castlemaine.

Those brooding hours, the ones after midnight, three or four in the morning, when I lie awake, mind racing, unable to get back to sleep, that's when I most often lacerate myself about the crimes and misdemeanours of my life. It's when, sometimes, I recall the gall of my question, my smart-arsery. Years after Peep dies, what I said to her on that day continues to haunt me, even if with diminishing returns.

~

Early autumn. Peep invites me to her house for lunch. I pick her a bunch of flowers, arrange them into a posy and head out. The day is warm, though not as hot as the day we meet on the street.

Peep's is a naturally cool house whose moderate temperature is enhanced by trees that enable dappled light into the open living room and kitchen area. Because there is a gentle breeze, the sunlight flickers and dances against the walls and the floor.

We eat a modest lunch of sliced ham, salad, bread and cheese. At ease with each other, we talk and laugh and reminisce our way through our meal. Plenty of time is devoted to criticising the hell out of the current Coalition government.

'Tea?' Peep asks.

When she returns from the kitchen, she places one cup and saucer set in front of me, another at her place. She returns to the kitchen and comes back with some fruit and a plate of sweet biscuits – two each. 'Now,' she says, 'it's time to talk about the elephant in the room.'

'Elephant?'

'Yes, your father,' she replies. And waits.

'You don't have to. I told you then, it's none of my business.'

'Perhaps, but I want to talk to you about him. About him and me.'

Butterflies are fluttering wildly in my stomach. 'OK.'

Dad and Peep were very fond of each other, she tells me, friends, comrades, collaborative peace workers. Theirs was an on-again, off-again affair. It went on that way for years, most often when Mum was suffering from severe back trouble or when she was recovering from spinal and other surgeries; also when things between my parents weren't going so well. And yes, times in between.

As she speaks, Peep watches me closely, waiting, I presume, for my reaction. But there is no reaction. What Peep tells me is detail; at the time I first realise there is an affair going on between them it doesn't bother me and it doesn't bother me now.

'It was just one of those things that happened,' Peep says. 'We enjoyed ourselves together. There were no strings, so we just kept going.'

There is little more to say than that. There is no more I want to know.

We pick away at the bunches of grapes, finish the biscuits and drink our tea, talking amiably. As I stand to leave, Peep hands me a plastic bag. 'Bearded iris rhizomes,' she says. 'I know you like them.' This fact emerges during one of our cafe conversations. 'They're white.'

We hug goodbye. Slowly, I walk the kilometre or so from her house to mine.

~

We continue to meet, mostly in cafes, though once at my house for lunch. Occasionally, we talk on the phone. Then, perhaps a year after our lunch at her house, Peep's health begins to fail. In time her family moves her to a pleasant aged-care facility in town, where some time later she dies.

Friends are invited to join Peep's family at an afternoon event to say their farewells. Although I attend, I find myself struggling to stay. My tears are, I'm aware, not only for Peep; they are also for Mum, who died two years earlier, and for Dad too, for all three of them and the intertwining of their lives.

~

Some time later, I decide to look her up, to see if there is an online entry for her in which I'll learn things I do not know but might like to. I get only as far as her obituary. Peep dies, I learn, on my birthday. Not being one for superstitions, this fact gives me pause all the same. In some way that I am unable to explain, it feels as if all four of us – Peep, Dad, Mum, me – are permanently linked, though I also know that even if she'd died on any other day, this would still be so.

Reflections after a Brief Correspondence with Kim

How goes the muse at your end? Kim writes. I am down to the wire, with Wednesday CoB the cutoff. Should be OK but exhausting. If all goes to plan would you like to have lunch with me Friday? My shout.

⌒

Thanks, I reply to my friend. I'd love to go to lunch. Today the muse has deserted me and the piggy eater has stepped up. I hate the piggy eater. I hate the story I am trying to write. Not enough courage, so the story reads stiff.

⌒

Coincidentally, a day or two later, I read a piece written by Vivian Gornick, a New York critic and essayist I have much admired since 1993 when I discover *The Romance of American Communism* in New York's erstwhile East 9th Street Bookshop. In this piece, Gornick cites another author, an autobiographical novelist who says 'You have to write about your friends and family as if they are dead,' or words to that effect, advice Gornick practises, particularly in *Fierce Attachments*, her book about her combative relationship with her mother.

To write this way requires an enormous amount of courage. Do I have it? Don't know that I do. Do I agree with her? Don't know that I do. Is it courage that's being discussed here? What role does loyalty play?

∼

Author Morris Lurie was scathing: 'If people don't like my version of events, let them write their own.' Morris gave no quarter.

∼

When a respectable amount of time passes after Mum dies – and ten years after Dad – my friend Hattie says, 'Now they're both dead, you can write anything you like. You don't have to be scared of them anymore.'

'Maybe,' I reply, 'but what about the mother and father who still reside in my head?'

'That's what you do your fucking therapy for,' says Hattie. 'Get rid of them.'

∼

Hattie's exhortations notwithstanding, I remain hamstrung by loyalty, a key ingredient of Goldbloom family life. By and large this loyalty attaches itself to Dad, in many quarters loved, admired, revered, just as in others he is equally reviled for his Left-wing views and his denial of

Soviet antisemitism. Criticisms are given heft by ongoing Cold War hostilities, more still by his persistence in holding the Soviet line against all comers. Not that he's a one-man band; he's not, but he is, without doubt, one of the staunchest band members. One of the loudest trumpets, you could say.

When people disagree with him, even close family friends who agree with his politics to greater or lesser extent, Mum appears loyal to her husband. Fiercely loyal. Ruthless, though, in her criticisms behind closed doors, where, without mercy, she hammers home her many contradictory views and lacerating criticisms.

~

It is possible that there is something else that hamstrings me in the writing, as it does in conversations. Despite years – which will become decades – of therapy, fear of my parents' disapproval remains deep within me; sometimes, even today, it bubbles to the surface. Will I get into trouble? Always getting into trouble, Sandra.

Without doubt, Mum would disapprove. Once, when I ask her advice about how to respond to questions about Dad's Party membership, her reply is terse. 'Just tell them he's not,' she snaps. 'That's what I do.'

~

It is also possible that there is yet another something. What if, contrary to Hattie's urgings, to Morris' wisdom, I don't want to kill off the parents in my head, the frequently punitive, authoritarian father, the frequently critical and disparaging mother, at least not completely?

149

What if that Dad, who I feared as much as I loved and admired, has receded enough into time and memory that he no longer has power over me? What if my affection for him increases with the years, leaving me to feel – to continue to feel – that to admit his Party membership to others is a form of betrayal? Or a regurgitation of the same old disloyalty? What if that?

~

As agreed, Kim and I meet for lunch. We do not talk about private revelations and disloyalty. We do have an enjoyable and interesting conversation while sharing a bowl of dumplings and a dish of noodles topped with pieces of crispy boneless chicken dressed with a piquant sauce. Kim pays for the lunch.

~

After I leave St Kilda and move to Castlemaine, Chris, a woman I knew in Melbourne, takes me under her wing. She invites me to come with her to Wesley Hill Market on Saturday mornings. Here, each week I meet market regulars, people from Castlemaine and surrounding hamlets, many of them refugees from Melbourne's inner city, a few from the suburbs, fewer still who have grown up here.

Chris makes the introductions: 'This is Sandra Goldbloom Zurbo.' During the first six months of my weekly market attendance, there are few Saturdays when someone doesn't respond: 'Are you related to that communist, Whatshisname Goldbloom?' or 'Wasn't your dad the boss of the Communist Party in Australia?' or 'Is that communist Sam Goldbloom your father?'

Most often I laugh at their questions, scoff at the elevation they ascribe to him – '*Boss* of the Communist Party?'

Who are these people? I don't know them, nor they me. They didn't know Dad. Or did they? Reverting to past comfort, to past *loyalty*, I reply with that long ago devised response, even though he's now fifteen years dead: 'He's always denied that he was a member of the Communist Party.' It is unlikely that many – any – of them believe me any more than did the people in the city who asked the same question.

One man gasps with what appears to be admiration, as if he's met the daughter of a rock star. Close quarters. In fact, he seems so taken with the proposition that I am *that* Sam Goldbloom's daughter he asks twice. 'You're Sam Goldbloom's daughter? Really? Sam *Goldbloom*'s daughter?' From his tone, from the shine in his eyes, from the crescendo in the upward inflection of his question, I take it that, for him at least, being Sam Goldbloom's daughter gives me cache.

~

Julie, a woman I have never met, asks a mutual friend if I am Sam Goldbloom's daughter. She remembers that Dad comes to a Richmond Communist Party branch meeting at her parents' house when she is a child. All the years since, Julie believes he must have been a Richmond branch member. Richmond is never his branch. He doesn't have a branch. As a secret member, he meets with Party apparatchiks at home or, most often, in cafes in the city, away from eavesdropping ears. At least officially, he continues to keep his membership secret. Most likely he attends the Richmond branch to give a talk about peace, nuclear disarmament or the conference he most recently returned from, just as he addresses many branches of the Communist Party, the Labor Party, peace groups, schools, church groups, factory shop floors, waterside workers and seamen. Anyone who invites him. Anyone who will listen.

What does she know, this stranger? What does she remember? A meeting is set up by our mutual friend.

〜

Julie and I meet for coffee with our friend the go-between. For the most part, we talk about art. Even when we get around to what she might know about Dad, little is to be learnt. All she remembers is that when she is eight years old Dad comes to her house, that he is very tall and that he likes children, which, as she has no siblings and there are no other children in the house at that time, must mean that he likes her.

In a couple of weeks, I will go to her house for lunch. Only the two of us will be there. Perhaps then there will be more gold to mine.

〜

There is not. Julie reiterates the same recollections as those the day we meet for coffee, after which we have a tasty lunch and a wide-ranging conversation that lasts for two and a half hours.

The lunch and the company, which includes her partner, are enjoyable. Nonetheless, I leave Julie's house feeling dissatisfied.

〜

Loudon Wainwright III: Surviving Twin. When I learn this film is streaming, I watch it because, by coincidence, earlier that afternoon

I enjoyed listening to him singing on the radio. I wouldn't call myself a fan, I don't seek him out, but when I come across his music, more often than not I enjoy listening.

The film is not what I expect. Yes, there is an audience in what, in the dim light, appears to be an old theatre. Yes, his guitar is on a stand next to a chair, and yes, nearby is a piano with what looks to be a ukulele case on top of it. Yet Wainwright's performance is not so much a concert as a ninety-minute monologue interspersed with a few songs of his own composition. He recounts his relationship with his father, and his father's with his father, Loudon's grandfather. Bastards all, it seems, including our narrator.

From the start, Wainwright lashes out at his brutal and disapproving father. As I listen, as I watch, a tremor passes through me. *He* has the requisite courage. *He* is not troubled by loyalty. Loudon Wainwright III struts back and forth on the stage before his audience, unafraid, somewhat arrogant. His apparent ability to publicly talk away the ghosts (or talk to them) is, he points out, the result of years and years of therapy.

Years of therapy notwithstanding, Loudon Wainwright III sounds bitter, snide. His late-age bitterness makes me dislike him. Were I ever to listen to his songs again, neither he nor they will ever sound as enjoyable as they have up until this night.

∼

Regardless of my own years of therapy, I remain unwilling to divulge family secrets, including my own. How much is one obliged to divulge? How much are others entitled to know? Who is entitled to know? Not everything, I conclude, and not everyone. Sometimes no one.

'Sandy,' Dad would sometimes say, 'if you want something to remain secret, keep it to yourself.' Correct.

Some things remain – must remain – private.

Should the people who so admired Dad be allowed in, to bear witness to his darkness, those aspects of him previously unrevealed that have nothing to do with his not so secret membership of the Communist Party? Why would I be the one to give more fuel to his critics, who, even to this day, continue with their detractions and denunciations? No, not everything needs be told. Not all the cone of silence confidences entrusted by family members, by friends, by comrades. After all, who tells everything? Every single thing?

Yet here I am, telling, confirming.

And here too, this: even now, I don't want to imagine his disapproval. Nor do I want to imagine my mother's criticism, addressing me with that disapproving voice she could muster at will, the voice that comes hissing out of tightly pursed lips. There are times when their voices ring out from inside my head, from the depths of our collective past, and refuse to be silenced.

Can it ever completely end, this need for approval? The die has long since been cast, so the best to be hoped for is spells – long, short – spells of alleviation, modification, an easing of the soul.

I will continue this conversation with my friend.

Kim, I write, things to talk about. Lunch on Thursday? My turn to shout.

Santamaria the *Mamzer*

Saturday, midmorning. I pick up some coffees and visit my parents. We sit around the table in their sun-filled dining room. After divvying up *The Age*, each of us begins to read our preferred section.

Dad reads the world news and articles about St Kilda Football Club. Mum, a compulsive gambler, checks the form guide in *The Sun*, then the Tattslotto results, before opening up *Good Weekend* and heading to the recipes page. I begin work on *The Age* puzzles, starting with the Target, segueing into the cryptic, and moving on to the general knowledge puzzle.

Amicably, peaceably, we sit around the table, sipping our coffees and eating Mum's biscuits, which she brings out of the pantry and arranges on plates. Every now and again, when Mum or Dad say, 'Hey, listen to this,' the other two look up from the pages we're reading or puzzling over and listen to what the other has found, an item they think might be of interest. It often is, though sometimes not.

'Here you go, Sammy,' Mum says. Smiling, she leans across the table to hand him the *Good Weekend*, folded over so only a single page is open to him.

'What've you got there, Rosie?' He smiles at her, but as soon as he sees what she's handed him, rage and contempt swipe away his smile. His expression hardens. 'Santamaria,' he growls, 'that *mamzer*.' Bastard.

'Let's see,' I say.

I've never met B A Santamaria, virulent anticommunist, staunch Catholic, leader of the Democratic Labour Party (the group that breaks away from the Australian Labor Party, which is why they are called 'Groupers' by people who despised them). The full-page colour photo that accompanies the feature article looks complimentary, generous. Santamaria seems relaxed, untroubled. He is wearing an open-necked shirt and a V-neck jumper, probably wool or cashmere.

Since the DLP's inception in 1956, Santamaria has been the bête noire of most Australian Labor Party members, former Communist Party members and members of every other Left-wing organisation in the land. Dad is one of the legion who has never forgiven Santamaria and his Groupers for what came to be referred to as the Split, which ALP members and their supporters believe caused the Labor Party to remain in the political wilderness for years.

Now it's my turn to grin. 'Why don't you get in touch with him, Dad?' I say.

Incredulous, he looks up from staring at the *Good Weekend* and glares at me. 'What?' he shouts. 'Are you mad? Why in hell would I do that?'

Out of the corner of my eye I can see Mum grinning.

'Two old warhorses, one of the Left, the other of the Right. You could sit in your recliner rockers and have a chat over a cup of tea. You'd probably have plenty to talk about.'

By now Mum and I are grinning ear to ear.

'I wouldn't talk to that *mamzer* if …' He sputters, momentarily unable to finish the sentence. 'I would *never* speak to him. *Never.* He wrecked the ALP. Split it. He and his bloody DLP Groupers were responsible for keeping the ALP out in the cold for years. Talk to him? Bugger that.'

After a bit more huffing and puffing, he hands the *Good Weekend* back to Mum and returns to his sports pages to see who the St Kilda lineup will be for this week.

Never would, never did.

～

Some time after both their husbands die, Mum and Mrs S happen to be at the same function, an afternoon tea. So many years have passed since the event Mum can no longer remember where it occurred or what the occasion was.

Although the two women have never met, Mum recognises Mrs Santamaria, who, she feels sure, recognises her. The two women acknowledge each other with a nod.

'If you'd never met, how did you know it was her?'

'I don't know,' she replies. 'I must have seen a photo of her in a newspaper or the *Women's Weekly*. Something like that.'

'Well, how would she have known who you were?'

'I don't know.' She is becoming irritated. 'Whatever it was, we both knew who the other one was.'

Neither woman makes any attempt to speak to the other. Mum never sees Mrs Santamaria again.

Three Gongs

Gong 1

Guests are visiting when I arrive at Mum and Dad's house. 'Come and look at these,' he says, grinning. He shows me three letters, each written by an antiwar colleague, two of them personal friends. Each letter, an accolade in its own right, nominates him for an Order of Australia Medal for his antiwar work. If he is accepted, his OAM will be endowed for an inaugural category.

On the queen's birthday weekend of 1990, medal winners are announced. Dad gets a gong. He could not be more thrilled, more proud.

A vitriolic editorial in the *Jewish News* expresses its disgust that a man who – all evidence to the contrary – denies the existence of antisemitism in the Soviet Union should be so honoured. Too excited to be much bothered, all he says on reading the editorial is 'Feh'. Then he picks up the phone to speak with one of his many friends and movement colleagues who call throughout the day to congratulate him.

We agree, Mum, Dad and I, that we will go together to Government House for the gong ceremony.

~

On the day his medal is presented, my parents, casually dressed but to the nines all the same, come by my apartment to pick me up. I am similarly dressed. Recipients and their families gather at Government House. The Goldblooms take their seats in the middle of a row in the middle of the room.

When his name is called, he walks purposefully to the front. Mum and I watch on, our heads swollen with pride.

Samuel Mark Goldbloom, whose OAM medal is pinned on his lapel by Governor Davis McCaughey, is the first person in Australia to be presented with an award for antiwar activities.

~

Gong 2

Many years after his death and not long after Mum's, a woman from Canberra emails. She writes that a new suburb is being built in the nation's capital. Molonglo Valley is to be its name. Streets in Molonglo are to be named after activists and reformers, a new category of street names. *We are considering naming one of the streets after your father,* she tells me.

Goldbloom Street, Molonglo Valley, Australian Capital Territory.

First I must confer with my sisters, I reply. When I do, neither seems especially interested, so I return the woman's email to say, *Thank you, I am delighted, please go ahead.*

Some years have passed since the naming. I haven't yet been to Canberra to see Goldbloom Street, and it's unlikely I'll get there. Really though, it's not the seeing that matters to me. What most pleases me is knowing it's there.

~

Gong 3

Michael Hamel-Green gets in touch. A once was Vietnam draft refuser, imprisoned for his resistance, Michael is now a retired academic. We haven't seen each other for a good thirty years. At one point after the war's end, we become neighbours when Michael and his wife, Fran, buy a house that backs onto the opposite side of the North Fitzroy lane to my house.

Michael writes to say he would like to visit me in Castlemaine. He has been asked to write an entry on Dad for the *Australian Dictionary of Biography* but in order to do so he needs to flesh out some of the information he has. Would it be alright to come to talk with me?

I am just as pleased to hear from Michael as I am that Dad will be recognised in this way. After a few emails back and forth, we settle on a date, agree on a time.

In one of our phone exchanges, Michael reminds me that he, together with others, went with Dad as a member of an Australian delegation to the Soviet Union. Not for the first time Michael tells me what a good time he had, what a charming host and tour guide Dad was. The trip, Michael says, is one of the highlights of his life.

~

A scorching hot mid-summer Saturday morning. Table's set, shakshuka is ready, everything but the eggs, which I will cook once we get settled. Kettle's full and ready to go. Then, it's 9.30 and there he is: the old draft resister is knocking at my door.

What a pleasure it is to see him. Michael has put on weight, as have I; his hair colour has changed, as has mine. But our enjoyment of a conversation remains unaltered. Once the eggs are ready, we sit at the table, eating, talking, reminiscing, exchanging views about the state of the world and activism today. Michael is more optimistic about the future than I am, much more. We finish our breakfast, I make coffee, then, Michael is ready to get going with the interview.

Although there is nothing he asks or that I can tell him that isn't in this book, I do enjoy hearing my responses out loud, appreciate the renewal of a friendship, and take pleasure in the reason Michael is here.

Now? Now I await, with keen anticipation, the publication of the twentieth volume of the *Australian Dictionary of Biography*.

Sammy and Rosie
Go to the Movies

He phones me. Before he says more than a couple of words, it is clear that he is entertained by something. He is already chuckling.

'Your mother and I ...' chuckle, chuckle, 'we're going to the movies this afternoon.'

'Yes?' Why does this make him so excited? Nothing new here.

'We're going to see *Sammy and Rosie Get Laid,*' he says, chortling now.

It takes a minute for the penny to drop. When it does, I begin to laugh too. I have read a review of Stephen Frears' film. It sounds good. In the background, I can hear Mum is also laughing.

~

They go to an afternoon session, which they enjoy immensely. Mum tells me, somewhat shyly, that they hold hands during the screening.

Weeks will pass before either parent is able to mention the title of this film without laughing with childlike delight.

Poetry

Sandra was one of the most precocious young girls ... she was reciting pieces of poetry at nine years of age and doing all the sort of hand motions that went with it ...

Sam Goldbloom, from a 1994 interview

~

Sometimes he recites poetry to me.

There was a little girl,
who had a little curl
right in the middle of her forehead.
When she was good
she was very good
but when she was bad
she was horrid.

At the end of this recitation, particularly if it's delivered during one of my supposed horrid periods, he usually sighs, long and loud, and slowly shakes his head from side to side. 'What am I going to do with you, Sandra?'

More than thirty years after his last recitation of 'There was a little girl', and twenty years after I have become a feminist, I decide to reciprocate, not with recitation, but by sending him a book. On a shopping expedition at St Mark's Bookshop in New York's East Village, I buy a copy of Maya Angelou's *Phenomenal Woman*. Powerful material jumps off its pages. The day after I finish reading it, I stroll over to the East 14th post office with the book in my backpack, stand in line until it's my turn at the window and post it to him.

Because I have an abiding faith in Australia Post's performance of its duties, I am certain his lack of acknowledgement of my gift has nothing to do with the postmaster's inefficiency. No, that is not the reason for his silence.

～

A couple of months later, when I arrive back in Melbourne and visit my parents, I ask him, 'Did you receive the book I sent you?'

'Book?' he says, feigning forgetfulness. 'Oh, the book.'

'Yes, the book. Did you like it?'

There is a slight pause. He is deciding whether to be forthright or diplomatic.

'Rubbish,' he says. 'Couldn't stand it. Why did you send me something like that?'

I grin, broadly. 'Payback,' I say.

Perplexed would be the most apt description of his expression in this moment. 'For what?'

'For all those "There was a little girls".' My grin is stretched across my face. 'And because I actually did think you might enjoy it.'

He pauses, then he shakes his head in wonder. Could he really have raised a daughter as misguided as this one?

'Where is it?' I ask.

'Where is it?' Again he pauses. Again forthright wins the day, after a fashion. 'I gave it away,' he says.

No point in asking to whom, though I suspect he donated it to the rubbish bin.

Ah well, point made, point taken – I think.

Launching *Rachel*
(Lazarus Rises)

My novel, *The Book of Rachel*, is accepted by a publisher. In the family there is considerable excitement and many mazel tovs. The novel is not the first of my published writing, but it is the first novel. My height feels as if it has increased by at least a metre.

~

Writing completed, contract signed, the production process begins.

The publisher engages the services of an editor, a designer and a typesetter. The typescript is given to the editor. The design, along with the file containing the book, is given to a typesetting house that will convert the typescript into pages. Two copies of the pages are produced on laser printer: one set each for the editor and the author, me. This is the time for last-minute changes, repairs, corrections, minor additions. The editor incorporates the author's markup into her copy and passes the work back to the typesetter, who takes in the corrections. Then, the amended copy is printed out for the proofreader.

For *Rachel*, an extra set of laser pages is printed. The publisher knows Dad is in one of his on the brink states. She thinks – quite rightly – he might like to read it before he dies (although she doesn't say 'before he dies', we both know that's what she means), particularly as it will still be some months before the book is printed, bound, boxed, delivered into distribution centres and, from there, to bookshops around Australia.

The publisher is correct. Dad is very ill so I'm very grateful she gives me this copy for my parents to read. What I most hope for is that he will live long enough to see the book properly printed and to attend the launch. Will he make it?

~

Do not *ask him how he's going with his reading.*
   Do not *ask what he thinks about the book.*
   These instructions are what I commit to.

~

One afternoon, about a week or so after I give him the laser printout, I go to visit.

'How are you going, Dad?'

'Not too bad today, thanks Sandy,' he replies.

'How about you, Mum?'

She makes a mock grimace and says, 'I'm fine thanks dear.'

Barely five seconds pass before I say: 'How are you going with the book, Dad?'

He smiles, Mum smiles. 'It's good, Sandy,' he says.

'What do you think?'

'He keeps saying how good it is,' says Mum, adding, 'I haven't read it yet.'

'It's really good, but …' I hold my breath while his face takes on what resembles a puzzled frown, 'reading a book that has a character in it that's based on yourself …' His voice trails off. 'It's strange, but I like it.' Although he gently shakes his head from side to side as if mystified, he is smiling.

'And?'

'And it's pretty damned good.'

We all laugh.

~

There is to be a launch at Readings. I could not be more anxious. Mum phones to ask if I'd like them to pick me up.

When they arrive, I see that, as ever, they are wearing dressy casual. I am wearing my finest New York bohemian: black trousers, black jumper (crew neck), black silk scarf, red leather ankle boots and black socks. Over the clothes a black woollen New York coat that stops about 15 centimetres short of my ankles; the collar is upturned. Around my neck is a necklace of large red glass beads I bought in New York. As well, I am wearing a pair of gold earrings and dark red lipstick. I clamber into the back seat and pull my coat in behind me.

Some squabbling ensues about whether this direction or another is the best way to get to Carlton, which route is likely to have the least traffic to navigate, which too many trams. Finally, after what feels like an eternity, a route is agreed upon and we set off.

~

Just as when we used to leave early for the airport to await Dad's departure for his overseas travels, we leave my apartment block with plenty of time to change a flat tyre should we need to or to call and wait for the RACV – we should live so long – should that need arise.

Such is the extent of my anxiety that were a feather to drop onto the seat beside me I would leap up and shoot straight out through the roof. I am so nervous, so wired, so sure I'll make a fool of myself … that no one will like my book … that no one will show up … Every time Mum speaks, every time she attempts to lighten my mood, to make conversation, I bite her head off, snap at her, growl loudly, tell her off. My anxieties are exacerbated because ever since both parents gave up cigarettes they have introduced a no smoking in the car rule. I am desperate for a smoke.

About two-thirds of the way to Carlton, a red light pauses our progress.

'Sandy,' Dad says, peering in the rear-view mirror at me, 'don't speak to your mother like that please. Settle down.'

'Sorry, Mum.'

'What's wrong with you? Why are you behaving like this?'

'I'm terrified,' I tell them.

'What for?' Dad is astonished.

From the back seat I can see in the mirror that his eyes keep darting from me to the lights as he waits for the change to green.

'I just am. I don't want to make a dill of myself. Everyone watching. Worst still, what if no one shows up?' I pause, then, 'Maybe no one will like the book.'

Exasperated, Mum laughs. 'Oh, for goodness sake.'

'Sandra,' Dad says, with one last glance in the mirror before the light changes and he begins to drive forward, 'who's coming to this event?'

169

'No one.'

'For chrissake,' Mum says. 'Stop it.'

'Cut it out,' says Dad. 'Seriously, it's family, friends, people who care about you, yes?'

'Yes.'

'All of them wish you well, yes? That's why they'll be there. They want you to succeed. Just take it easy.'

'I suppose,' I mumble.

'Suppose.' In the mirror I see him roll his eyes. 'Look, here's a little trick to help you. This is something I do if I'm feeling a bit nervous about speaking.'

'You?'

'Yes, sometimes I get nervous too,' says the man I know as a fearless public speaker.

'What do you do?'

'I try to find one person I know, preferably know well, someone I trust. Then I fix my eyes on them and talk directly to them.'

'What if no one like that is there?'

'Unfortunate, but if there's not, I cast my eyes just a little bit above people's heads.'

Mum intervenes. 'Just find your father and look at him,' she says.

Dad nods his agreement. 'That's it. Just look at me.'

We drive on.

~

Ralph Gibson, short, wiry, stern, unassuming to look at, early member of the Communist Party of Australia is a fiery public speaker who can be heard championing the cause on Sundays at the Yarra Bank, a speakers corner across the road from the Yarra River, near where Rod Laver Arena now stands. Ralph sometimes comes to our house to have a quiet meeting with Dad. I never get to know him particularly well, even though he is still alive at the time I join the Party.

Ralph and his physical opposite, family friend Judah Waten, who is as tall as Dad and much more solid, scare me with their stern looks, Judah in particular with his booming voice, his heavy black eyebrows that don't quite meet in the middle, who looks to me through my teenage years to be an aged Reggie, a character in the Archie and Jughead comics.

Some years after Ralph dies, my friend and comrade David tells me Ralph was a very shy man, that it was a feat for him to get up on a soapbox to address a Sunday-afternoon Yarra Bank crowd, even to address meetings of the faithful. So much so, David tells me, that Ralph practised his speeches in front of a mirror, not only for timing but also for confidence.

What a shock that was.

In preparation for my book launch, I put my knowledge of Ralph's timing rehearsals to good use. Not that I stand in front of a mirror, but I do use a timer to help whittle down the thank-you part of the speech I am going to make before reading, and to help trim down that portion of the book I'll read.

~

My mother is a lucky parker. Pick any thoroughfare or carpark, there will always be a parking spot in front of, or no more than two or three spots away from, where she needs to be. It's as if the previous parker knows she is on her way and obliges by leaving just at the time she arrives so the space might not be grabbed by someone else. It is likely the one element of her gambler's life in which she is, without fail, a winner.

Along with most of her physical ailments and several elements of her personality, or variations of them, this luck in finding a parking spot is my inheritance from her. My daughter tells me that she also has the gift. We Goldbloom women? Lucky parkers, that's us.

Dad finds a park on Lygon Street, two spaces away from Readings.

'How about this?' he exclaims, delighted, as if he secures the space off his own bat. Neither Mum nor I say a word.

We have arrived with more than twenty minutes to spare.

'I'm going to Tamani to have a stiff coffee and a smoke before I come inside,' I tell them. I get out of the car as quickly as I can, light up the cigarette I have at the ready and walk off up Lygon Street. 'Won't be long.'

'Sandra, where are you going?' A friend spots me striding away from the bookshop.

'Coffee and a smoke to settle my nerves. I'll be there soon.'

Two double-shot espressos and two cigarettes later, I fix my lipstick, step out onto the street (it's busy tonight, a lot of people around), shake off my nerves and turn up my coat collar. Then, book in hand, I walk back to the bookshop.

At the door, just before I go in, I take two deep breaths and fluff up my curls. With a smile pasted on my face, I stride through the shop, greeting friends and family as I move to the back area where the launch is to be held.

～

The shop is packed. Goodwill emanates from all the people I thought – feared – were not going to be here.

The publisher speaks first, then the bookshop owner, who tells the gathered how long he and I have known each other (around twenty-five years), and then the book is launched by my friend Sal, herself a former publisher, who comes from Canberra to launch it.

Then it is my turn.

It works, his trick, particularly as he is not at all difficult to find in the crowd: my parents are seated not far from the podium.

After disposing of the formalities, thanking the appropriate people, I say how glad I am to have so many of my family here tonight – especially glad, I say as I look directly at him, that old Lazarus is able to be here for the liftoff. He smiles. Indeed, smiling and soft chuckling ripple through the room. Most everyone here knows Dad, knows he is dying, knows how much I care about him.

Mum is also smiling; gently, she nods. No question about how glad she is that he's here for this event, that he's still here at all.

~

Formalities over, books bought and signed, a mob of about a dozen of us go to dinner. My parents leave earlier than everyone else; a friend drives me home. A good time is had by all.

Three weeks later, Dad is back in Cabrini, tap tap tappin' on heaven's door.

The Massage

Seated on the end of the hospital bed, I contemplate his feet. Dry, scaly, the ankles bloated with fluid. Thorny little spikes of skin poke out at wild angles from around the rim of his heels. His long big toe puts me in mind of a sad-sack character in a children's storybook. Toe Man. Sad old Toe Man.

I take his foot and cradle it between my warm hands. 'Cold,' I remark, discomfited by the prickliness, repulsed by the thick, chilly flesh. His leg is a dead weight. I release his foot.

'They are always cold. No circulation, they tell me. Ever since the surgery.'

I do not enquire which surgery: it is unlikely we will agree. We would grow irritated with each other. Eventually, we would bicker.

In the past six years, there have been many surgeries. At first they were performed as couplets: angioplasty – two; removal of gangrene – two; prostate cancer – two. More recently, a triple bypass due to angina, followed ten days later by a single heart attack. 'His first,' was how the medical staff put it at the time.

Excision of …

Sometimes I imagine he will leave us by stealth, disappeared, one small body part at a time.

⁓

The cuffs of his pyjamas have come to rest – or are they hitched up? – midway on his calf muscles, which have grown slack from infrequent use.

He is miserable today. I would like to cheer him up. I would like – as ever – to please him. 'Would you like me to massage your feet?'

His swift response does not surprise me, not in the least. 'Yes please.' At once he begins to wriggle himself into a position of greater comfort. 'That would be nice.' He clears his throat.

'You know,' he begins, ordering his thoughts, as though he were recounting the story for the first time, 'when I travelled I had many different sorts of massage …'

A list of foreign capitals is rattled off, large towns are named, and the massage variations he experienced in them: on tables, futons, mats. (He does not – ever – mention beds, which does not stop me from wondering.) With the passing of time it has become more problematic for him to recollect precisely. Berlin for …? What was it in Berlin? In Rome, a woman – or was it a man? Prague? Ah, Prague. His sighs wistfully but does not elaborate. Leningrad? Ah yes, Leningrad – in Leningrad, he recalls, there was rigour. Oy, how his flesh was pummelled! He smiles, then worries at the inside corner of his lower lip with his incisors. Or was that Barcelona? He stops chewing his lip. No, he is adamant now: Leningrad. A man from Barbados in London. Hanoi … hmm, light, feathery hands, he recollects.

'Cups!' he exclaims. Bamboo cups in Shanghai. He enjoyed the cups. In Haifa: chop chop chop chop. Rapid, strong, rhythmic. 'No,' he pauses, 'now that I think of it, the chopping might well have been ...'

He purses his lips and frowns. It is a small frown, expressing frustration at his diminishing ability to make matching pairs of treatments and cities.

~

Listening – and not listening – to the Muzak of his voice as he meanders the world, I consider, once again, the colours in the ward.

They are bland. Nothing about them excites the senses. Pale. Everything pale: pink walls, beige seats, white sheets and curtains, pastel cotton-weave blankets. Even his pyjamas are pale. Faded powder blue. His favourite pair of faded powder blue pyjamas.

There is a stool, an ottoman, its frame constructed of tubular steel; the seat, grey leather. (Is it leather, or one of those clever vinyls that approximates the genuine article in appearance and texture?) Two commercial prints, bucolic in theme, hang on one wall: unimaginative works, they are rendered drearier still by the insipid colours depicting – where? Australia?

My black clothes and earthy red lipstick stand in stark relief. And there, on the bench opposite his bed, a cut-glass vase filled with freesias. Blooms the yellow of ripe corn. Garish.

A bronze Christ, twice crucified – once to the cross, once to the wall – hangs above his bald Jewish head. The son of God appears to be listening intensely, far more so than I, leaning forward, head to one side, as if attempting to catch every word of this yarn about international rubbings and unguents.

~

Dad's reminiscences have become tiresome. In Milan, I release his foot, turn from him and walk to the mirror, where I watch as my lips shape his words, as I mouth the intact fragments of his memories with him, grateful that he pays me no heed. That he is unable to see me. From bed to mirror, our lines of vision do not converge.

The pouches under my eyes seem more bloated than usual. As he continues his journey, massage by massage, I indulge my vanity. Using my index finger, I exert a gentle pressure on the puffiness beneath my left eye, moving the finger slowly along the inflated curve, a few millimetres at a time, until a full arc is completed. The cool touch of my finger against the overheated skin of my face feels pleasant, a welcome relief. In the background his voice continues, fluttering, a sea breeze rippling through muslin curtains.

'I even had a woman walk all over my back once. Imagine that!'

At last. There it is. The ending he so loves. He chuckles quietly. Years after the event – could it be twenty? Twenty years? – this portion of the tale continues to induce in him a boyish wonder, though at which particular aspect I have never known. That he had the audacity to permit such an act? But what would I, a mere daughter, know of this, his audacity or otherwise in matters of the flesh? He pauses to consider. 'Now, where was that? Singapore? No, I think that one must have been Kyoto.'

'You always said that one was in Tokyo, Dad.'

I turn from my haggard reflection and face him, just in time to see him cock an eyebrow. A little testily – only a little; we are on good behaviour with each other today – he says, 'Well then, it must have been Tokyo.'

Satisfied, he settles back into the bank of pillows and offers me his feet. 'Left first, or right?'

'Let's start on the right foot, Dad.'

~

Each element proves to be in perfect harmony with the other: my body seated on the ottoman with the height of the bed, the location of Dad's foot on the mattress with my hands and arms. Everything. No adjustments need be made.

A dazzlingly white towel is draped across my lap. While Dad makes himself comfortable, I rub my palm back and forth over the cotton, enjoying its coarse, luxuriant pile, and find myself wishing for towels like these for my own bathroom. But this texture of towelling seems only to be found in hospital wards.

Dad gives a cheeky little hitch to his pyjamas. I smile at this and, more sentimentally, at the silver wisps of what little is left of his hair, fanned out on the pillow, a display that gives him a soft, angelic appearance. An elderly angel.

He folds his hands one over the other and rests them on his stomach. Dissatisfied with this arrangement, he straightens his arms and places them alongside his body. Then he closes his eyes. He releases a sigh, an anticipatory quiver of breath. Dad is ready for his Australian massage to begin.

He looks to me to be laid out.

~

From a pump-action plastic bottle, I squeeze out a large dollop of hydrolysing cream, an odourless, viscous fluid, and smear it from one hand to the other. Above the pallid – no, white, I must say it, above the naked white, greyish white, the deathlike white – skin of his long legs, my hands, browned by the sun, divested of jewellery, are poised, hovering. Hovering.

In that moment my hands appear to me as birds, indecisive creatures, trembling with uncertainty. To go on, or fly off? Withdraw or remain? My cheeks burn; my skin begins to itch. My heart is racing.

Hovering hands, racing heart.

I wonder – cannot help wondering – if Dad is aware of it, this moment in which I have become afraid of what I have offered. Does he feel – as I do – a twinge of … impropriety? Yes, that's it. Impropriety. A certain lack of decency, to be massaging my father's feet. Indecent to be running my hands over his flesh. A transgression.

But for the shallow rise and fall of his chest, he does not move. Not so much as an eyelash, not one nervous twitch. He is in a state of serene anticipation. I imagine that if he notices anything at all it is that I have not yet begun my ministrations.

Hands hovering. Heart racing.

Too late now to withdraw. How could I possibly explain? 'Sorry, Dad. I have changed my mind. To touch you so is too unfamiliar. And too familiar.' Hardly. Whatever remark I were to make, it will embarrass us both.

∽

I avert my eyes from his body to a space on the wall – above his head and away from the suffering Christ. I work by feeling out the landscape, spreading a thick layer of cream over his foot and ankle. Stroke. Knead. Slide. Press. Around. Up. Down. Brisk, functional movements. Short, tentative strokes. More gingerly, I work over his leg, saved from any impropriety – from further impropriety – by the cuffs of his pyjamas, beyond which point I decline to venture. He twitches when I slip my fingers between his long, dry toes. An urge to tickle his sole rises in me. Promptly, and with decorum, the urge is repressed.

The moment has come when I must abandon the security of the wall. I need to pump more cream from the bottle. Looking at him is unavoidable. Besides, I have grown curious. Is he enjoying himself?

His eyes are still closed. It is safe to peer at him. The length of him, from his face, along his body to his legs and feet. All that remains of the coating of cream is a sheen; his foot, his shin, his slack calf muscle, are glistening with it.

Dad's breath is even. Is he asleep? How unusual to observe him in such repose. He is utterly at peace. Seeing him so, something shifts in me. It is a physical sensation. What a commonplace, to speak of a burdensome weight being lifted from the shoulders, yet that's precisely what I feel. There are no other words. My spine straightens, the knots in my shoulders and neck dissolve.

I smile at him. How desperately I sought his approval. Is this how compassion feels? Light, and suffused with love? With forgiveness?

～

I have always thought of him as a powerful figure, a robust, passionate man who would never be damaged, who would never become ill. He would never die.

Never die? No, not never. Never is inaccurate. He would die. Of course he would die. But later. Not this year, not next. Or the next. Later. Much later. One day. And wasn't that always his little joke?

'I don't have time to die,' he would say. 'There is too much I want to do yet. Still too much to see. There's a world out there that needs saving. No time to die.'

~

I sit on the ottoman, holding his swollen foot in my cream-soaked hands. Along his shins, against the pallor of whiteness, the finest of red and blue lines stand out – veins and arteries, dense reddish purple galaxies of burst blood vessels. His shins resemble a section of electronic wiring. Intricate. Delicate. A delicate fatherboard. Or are they the detail of a Jackson Pollock? *Number 9*, perhaps? *Number 1*? If I could paint, I would make art of his red and blue veins, his purple patches, set against the canvas of his white skin. Perhaps start a movement. Gather in all those women who wish to draw their aged male parent: skin, veins and arteries, limbs, balding pates, the signifying scars where organs and protuberances have been removed. Forlorn Toe Men. Dadism.

~

Maintaining a gentle hold on Toe Man, I walk around to the other side of the bed. I know a thing or two about massage: don't release the subject, maintain the energy flow. This is essential.

Do not let go.

'Just changing sides, Dad.' I whisper so as not to startle him.

He smiles and murmurs, 'Mmm.'

I am not going away, not deserting him.

~

I put my weight behind my arms and give them power. Movement becomes uninhibited, fluid. Sweep upwards, slide down, more pressure here, less there. Long, soothing strokes. Their soothing touches me, too.

The prickly tacks of skin soften; they become silky and lie down. Blood begins to circulate. Colour returns to his feet; their pinkness is delightfully childlike.

Beads of perspiration form on my upper lip; I lick them away. Without haste, so as not to disturb the rhythm – to minimise any disturbance to the rhythm – I lift my right arm to my forehead and use the sleeve of my blouse to brush away the sweat that has gathered there while I continue the flow of the massage with the left. He does not remark upon the absented hand. He is patient. Patient.

Three-quarters of an hour passes. I draw my hands down his leg, past his ankle to his toes and out into the air.

Soaring birds of hands. Soaring birds. Out into the air.

⁓

'Did you enjoy that?'

'Mmm, I did.' His speech is thick. 'Very much.' He pauses. 'Thank you.'

I have pleased him.

'Would you like me to come again tomorrow?'

He places an upturned hand on the bedclothes, an invitation to me to hold it. His hand, too, feels dry. Flaky. He wraps those elegant fingers around my hand, draws it to his lips, kisses my fingers. He nods. 'That would be lovely.'

'Goodbye then, Dad. See you tomorrow.'

Eyes locked, we smile at each other. I nod, take my leave and am almost out the door when I turn to look at him. In all likelihood his eyes have not left me.

'I love you, Dad.'

Quietly, I leave the room.

Another Lunch

We are on the phone.

'Dad,' I say, 'would you like me to pick you up and take you for a Vietnamese noodle soup?'

He knows I'm talking about I ♥ Phở, our favourite noodle shop in Richmond. A sucker for soup of any kind at any time of the year, and eager to leave the house for a while, he accepts my invitation. 'Thanks, Sandy. That would be great. When did you have in mind?'

On the day I arrive to pick him up he is not in great shape, but he insists we continue with our arrangement; he is very keen to eat Vietnamese soup noodles.

～

Victoria Street, bustling and teeming with people, seems particularly busy today. Finding a parking space close to the noodle shop will be impossible, so I park in an almost secret carpark, tucked in behind a group of shops that once was the Valhalla Cinema. Parking here means only a short walk to the cafe, around ten or so shops west.

We take off together, but after passing five shops, I realise he is no longer beside me, not even right behind me. Where is he? Being six foot three, although a little stooped these days, he isn't hard to spot above the crowd of mostly Vietnamese. There he is, leaning against a shop window, ashen, exhausted, gripping his walking stick for dear life.

Flushed with shame at having given no consideration to whether he can, in his weakened state, keep up, whether he can manage so crowded a street after the quiet of his home, I race back to him, apologetic that I haven't acknowledged his frailty.

When I reach him, he says, puffing, 'Do you always walk this fast?'

He takes my arm, and slowly, very slowly, we walk together past the remaining shops to I ♥ Phở. He asks me to order for him. 'One Phở bò, one Hanoi Phở gà,' I say to the waiter. Beef for Dad, chicken for me.

When the food arrives, he drinks a small amount of the broth, pushes the noodles around with his chopsticks in a desultory way, picks at a couple of slices of beef, then sets the chopsticks down on the table. 'Very tasty.' But his heart isn't in it.

Above the cafe's hubbub, his murmur is almost inaudible. 'Sandy,' he whispers after fifteen minutes at table, 'take me home please.'

I have him stay inside the cafe so he can be seated while he waits for me. 'I'll toot the horn when I'm outside.'

He nods, but says nothing.

I become anxious that a tram will come and I'll be blocking its way. The driver will *ding ding ding* me to hurry me along, which is not how I want to draw attention to myself. As well, I feel guilty because I've left Dad, so keen to get home, stranded in a bustling cafe.

185

My humiliation fantasy doesn't materialise. In fact, the reverse happens. Before I can exit the carpark, I must make way for a tram heading towards the city. After it moves on, I drive up to the noodle shop, *toot toot toot*, jump out of the car and fetch him from where he stands – just – outside the cafe door.

We drive home in silence. When we arrive, Mum, who is shocked to see him in this condition, gives me an admonishing glare as she helps him in through the front door. Tenderly, she says as she moves towards him, 'Come on, Sammy. How about a little lie down?' When she returns to the kitchen after helping him into bed, she says tartly to me, 'You should never have taken him.'

That is the last lunch we have together at I ♥ Phở. His next hospital admission is just around the corner. It is to be his last.

Moving Day

Dad likes to keep a tally of the number of times he's been admitted to hospital. 'This is my seventeenth time … my twenty-first … twenty-eighth …' Often, he sounds as if he is in a competition, a race, though with whom is unclear; most likely himself. *How many times can I be admitted and continue to live?* Yes, of course. That's what the competition is: a tussle with death, the outcome of which you wouldn't bother to put money on.

Still, his battle – against cancer, cardiovascular disease, medically induced diabetes, medically induced pethidine addiction – is impressive.

Number twenty-nine? It will be his last hoorah, albeit a feeble one.

~

Doctors and nurses at Cabrini are kind to him; they take good care of him. Among the medical staff are several who develop a great affection for him.

Some time well before his twenty-ninth admission, or 'visit', as I have begun to call them – just one example of the myriad ways one can deny the impending death of a loved one – I take to visiting him in the evening, usually around half past six, seven o'clock, when it is quieter, when most of the visitors, family and friends, have gone home and he has a reprieve from the ministrations of the nursing staff. It is when I have him to myself.

Mum, who comes to call this 'Sandra's time', lingers, waiting to see me for a moment. Then, exhausted from a long day of cooing and stroking, tending and keeping company, of speaking with doctors and nurses, of the performance at home earlier in the day of wifely duties and other generosities – making him chicken soup, laundering his pyjamas, shopping to satisfy his needs and desires – she leaves the room to return to their unit. Once at home, she repairs to the bedroom to change into her nightie and dressing gown, and slips on her pink brocade slippers, the left of which has a small, frayed hole at the big toe. Then she heads to the dining room, where she drops a couple of iceblocks into a tumbler, pours herself a whiskey and tops it up with water. Mum then sits in the armed chair at the dining table, flicks on the television and watches *SBS News*.

Occasionally, I visit Dad during the day, but the chatter, the competition for his attention, the comings and goings of the nursing staff, of Bernadette the pastoral care worker, the cleaning and food delivery staff, any other visitor, it all becomes unbearable.

We don't speak much. By admission twenty-nine he is too weak, too doped up to talk; he is always tired, always dozing. As a rule, I just sit, thinking about our lives: together, separately, the pleasures, the fun, the mutual admiration, the painful and angry times, the times when I hate him for the brutal and humiliating punishments he metes out for my misdemeanours small and large.

⁓

Most often he sleeps, sometimes waking briefly to smile, to wiggle a finger by way of greeting. Soon after he closes his eyes again, though I rarely know whether he is sleeping or just lying there with his eyes closed. Which is not at all the same thing.

It is disquieting to see him like this: subdued, barely able to move, not interested in anything but the smallest of small talk. Despite him always having been an extraordinarily large presence, here he is now, diminished, sad, depressed. Now he is still, unmoving. Now there are no opinions forthcoming, not about anything. Now he is dying.

~

One evening, on my way home from visiting Dad after he's been in the hospital for over a week, I drop in to see Mum.

'They want him to leave,' she says. A woman of strength – and pig-headed stubbornness – who rarely cries, she tells me this as large tears roll down her cheeks. 'They don't want someone there who's going to die. They want the other patients to keep their spirits up.' She sobs loudly. '*Mamzers*,' she hisses. 'Bastards.' When I hug her, the synthetic fabric of her gaudily printed floral blouse slithers against my arms. It makes my skin crawl.

~

Bethlehem palliative care hospice is, depending on the traffic, a five to fifteen minute drive south along Kooyong Road from where my parents live. Mum doesn't want Dad to be moved there; she wants him to stay in Cabrini, as do I, as do the sisters.

189

Mum and I are called to a meeting at the hospital to discuss the regulations that govern who stays, who goes and under what circumstances. Few of them I recall, and none of them now matter because, with the exception of one nurse, the nursing staff want him (re)moved; there is to be no further discussion about it.

~

On the day, I arrive early to spend some time with Dad before going to the meeting. When I walk into his room, the sight of him shocks me.

Sitting up, slouched to one side against a bank of wildly placed pillows, he is on the nod; his eyelids droop and flutter. His sparse silver hair is so dishevelled that it appears to be flying off his head in every direction. His chin is covered with silvery stubble, a clear indication he hasn't been shaved for a couple of days. Through the stubble, from a corner of his mouth, runs a thin line of drool. His pyjama jacket is awry. Only one button is done up, askew at that, so most of his chest is exposed. His once-flat, now pronounced, belly protrudes from the gap. The right sleeve of the pyjama jacket is on, the left dangles halfway around his back, leaving his arm exposed. Because the drawstring of his pants isn't properly tied, his pubic hair is also exposed.

His bedding, too, is a mess, rumpled and not tucked in.

He seems to sense my presence, hear my footfall. Perhaps I arrive just at the moment he raises his eyelids. When he greets me, his voice, once loud and commanding, a voice that addressed and riveted thousands at antiwar rallies and public meetings, is now a barely audible, whisper: 'H'lo, Sandy.' He works his lips into a wobbly line of a smile, revealing the absence of the false front tooth he acquires only six months earlier; the denture is sitting on the table, though not in a glass of water.

~

We are sitting at the dining table, Dad, Mum and me, enjoying dinner. Suddenly, Dad stiffens, spits something into his hand, inspects what it might be and throws the something across the room. It hits the teak buffet with a clunk.

'Fuck! Fuck! Fuck!' he shouts despairingly. 'There's going to be nothing left of me.'

A tooth has fallen out. It is the tooth that hits the buffet.

While he continues to rail and swear, Mum and I can see a gaping hole in the top row of his teeth.

'Fuck.' He throws his serviette down on the table, shoves his chair away, stands up and strides to the bathroom to survey the damage. 'Fuuuuuuck!'

~

By this time Dad is eating little of anything. Only the mushy sweet stuff – plastic tubs of custard, jellies, processed fruit – satisfies (perhaps) his notoriously sweet tooth. There was a time when he would have gobbled up the lot. Indeed, there would never have been a time when such an accumulation of desserts had a chance to occur. Now, on his table, near the tooth that would not, could not, eat them, is a Twelve Apostles of dessert tubs, one empty, three with a teaspoon or two eaten from them, the remainder untouched, not even opened. Three partially drunk glasses of water stand among the apostles.

~

'Got any more of that, Rosie?' he holds out his dessert bowl for a refill from the several on the table.

'Which one, dear?'

'Yeah, that one.' He grins broadly, as his outstretched hand hovers over the entire selection.

Worst sweet tooth in Melbourne. Dentist bills to prove it.

~

Mum enters the room. It is clear that she, too, is shocked by this miserable scene. She gasps, but neither of us says anything.

A nurse enters the room and, as if she realises she has come through the wrong door, makes an abrupt turn. Just before she is out of sight, I muster some courage: 'Please, could someone put Dad's pyjamas on properly, clean him up a bit? And clear away this mess?'

She stops and turns back into the room. 'We're pretty busy,' she replies, 'but as soon as someone's available …' Then she leaves.

Still seated, I slip his arm into his pyjama jacket, do up the buttons in an order that matches the buttonholes and run my fingers through his hair. As I stand up, Mum reaches for my hand and squeezes it. She removes a comb from her favourite handbag, a large shoulder bag of scarlet leather, and lovingly combs his hair. When she has finished, her expression becomes resolute. 'Right,' she says, and sets to. She gathers up the tubs of fruit, the custards and the jellies, and drops them all into a plastic rubbish bin that stands against the wall. She takes the three glasses of water into the bathroom and empties their contents into the basin.

'This is what I pay private health insurance for?' she sneers.

We each take a turn to kiss Dad goodbye, tell him we'll be back soon, and then, hand in hand, walk down the corridor to the room where the meeting is to take place.

I'll cut to the chase.

The nursing staff, with the exception of one who is outnumbered several times over, are adamant. As soon after this meeting as a bed becomes available, Dad is to be transferred from Cabrini to Bethlehem, a palliative care hospice.

~

Among the sisters, the fractiousness and shifting alliances that so often divide us evaporate. United we stand: we want to be a part of his care, part of his death, just as we have been part of his life.

We siblings want what Dad wants: for him to be at home when he dies. Here, with the help of the many inhome services available to war veterans, we, together with Mum, can look after him, take shifts around the clock and be with him until he dies.

Mum is more ambivalent. Before the decision is made for her by the hospital, she finds it impossible to make up her mind. Even though she seeks the opinion of each daughter in turn, individually and when we are together, it is likely she repeats this questioning in order to hear out loud the sound of her own feelings, to run them past herself.

Hospital pastoral care worker Bernadette – 'Just call me Bernie' – comes to talk to Mum about why it might not be such a good idea to have Dad 'pass away' at home, why the hospice would be a better place for him to be. When a bed becomes available, it would be wise for Mum to accept it.

Bernie is tall, trim, blonde. Her eyes sparkle. Bernie is not the first woman to be besotted by Dad, not by a long shot, though she is the last. 'Wants him for herself,' Sister Two snorts. Sister Two never likes Bernadette and refuses to call her Bernie. Sister Three is neutral about her, as Three is about many things.

Bernie and I become friends. We meet from time to time in the hospital canteen to have coffee together, occasionally a meal. Sometimes we talk on the phone. My friendship with Bernie continues this way for a few months, until one day, on an occasion I go to visit Dad at Cabrini, it comes to an abrupt end. It takes only a few minutes.

~

I arrive at the doorway of the ward to see her leaning over him in a manner that makes me feel as if I am intruding on a … something … a conversation between lovers, perhaps. He is lying flat out in the bed, she is perched on a chair alongside, her face close to his head. She appears to be whispering in his ear; her cheeks are flushed.

Anger overcomes me.

Do I gasp? Do I make some other sound that distracts her from this intimacy? I don't remember, but I do know that she looks up and smiles at me, apparently not at all fussed by my presence, though the shock on my face must be evident. Quietly, she holds up her hand to keep me at bay ('Stay', says the hand), then indicates with her fingers that she wants three more minutes.

That is the moment. Fuck you, Bernie.

As I move into the room, Dad lifts a feeble hand and waves me in. A look of displeasure flits across Bernadette's face, but she rises, greets me with a warmth I do not reciprocate and leaves the room.

'She was trying to bring me to Jesus,' he says, smiling. 'How are you today, Sandy?'

~

Here she is now, in Mum and Dad's lounge room, dressed to the nines, that schoolgirl flush on her cheeks, sipping tea, complimenting Mum on her biscuits – 'Mmm, delicious, Rosa' – as she speaks quietly but insistently to Mum about why it would be best for Dad to go from the hospital to Bethlehem rather than come home.

He will have around the clock care, she says. He will be more comfortable, she says. Afterwards, she says – here comes the clincher – it will be easier for Mum to live in the house if he were not to die here, this point relentlessly hammered home. We may visit him at Bethlehem any time of the day or night we want to, she says.

And so it comes to pass.

~

Only a few days after Mum and I meet with the Cabrini staff, we are advised to take advantage of the bed that has just become available at Bethlehem. There's room at the inn. He is to go that afternoon. Sisters Two and Three, having recently returned to Melbourne from their homes on the New South Wales coast, will stay with Mum for the duration.

On the day Dad is moved, it is agreed that the sisters, together with Mum, will drive from Cabrini to Bethlehem in Mum's car; I am to travel with Dad in the ambulance. We wait in the ward until the ambulance drivers have Dad loaded onto a gurney, then follow down the hall, into the lift and out the electronic doors into the ambulance parking bay.

No goodbyes forthcoming, none given.

~

As it happens, Dad is not the only passenger. A handsome, mobile woman, also in her late seventies, makes pleasant chatter until the ambulance men have Dad installed, after which she clambers in unaided.

Her neatly combed hair is silver, wavy (is it permed or a natural wave?), her dark pink, purple-tinged lipstick perfectly applied, as is her face powder. The varnish on her manicured fingernails matches the colour of her lipstick. On her wrinkled fingers, a collection of rings: a small diamond engagement ring, a wedding band, two eternity rings. Liver spots are spattered across the back of her hands, where her veins protrude. Otherwise, the woman's skin is creamy white. The ambulance is taking her back to her nursing home.

Irritated by her conviviality and the banality of her conversation, I turn away.

'Do you know,' this fetching woman says, addressing no one in particular, 'this is my twenty-ninth admission to this hospital?'

I whip around to look at her; she is beaming with pride.

There it is. Of *course*. She's in the same race as Dad. They are old, this woman, my father. All that silver – hair, whiskers, eyebrows, chest hair. Elderly. Drugs, equipment, all manner of potions and procedures prolong their lives. Of *course* it's not unusual for an elderly person to have been in hospital many, many times – twenty-nine times, more – a thought that deflates me as much as it satisfies me. As I sit there, waiting for the ambulance to depart, I contemplate just how much I've been running Dad's race too, how much I've been in the race with him, for him. C'arn, Dad, you can do it. Another year, another month, a week even, another hospital admission. Another lap of life. Come on. Come *on*. *Biz a hindert un tsvantsik*, Dad. May you live to be one hundred and twenty, as old as Moses when he died, which is what Dad always said he was going to be. It's how Jews greet family members of a deceased relative, or close friends. 'I wish you a long life. *Biz a hindert un tsvantsik.*'

~

Two things strike me about Bethlehem: it is very old and very dark. Bleak house. It is, I know, a cliché to say my heart sank, but it did. My heart sank. I felt it drop. After the bright, modern hospital, despite the poor treatment he receives in his last week there, it feels as though Dad has been cruelly consigned to a decrepit medical outpost to end his days. I bite hard on the inside of my cheek so as not to burst into tears, tears that are, I'm well aware, about more than my first impressions of what is to be Dad's last place of residence.

What we have learnt is that when a patient is moved to palliative care it means death is likely to occur within about ten days. Give or take.

Dying Night

Bethlehem stands on the corner of Kooyong Road and Saturn Street, Caulfield South. Saturn Street? Astrologically, Saturn, the task-master of the zodiac, represents masculine energy. Perfect. My life's taskmaster ends his own life on Taskmaster Street.

Bethlehem's ward windows face west and north. The Kooyong Roadside of the hospice is lined with plane trees that spread across the road to form a cavern. Dappled sunlight streams through their branches. Cars whoosh through the cavern, and occasionally – about every twenty minutes – a bus.

∼

The car is packed. Mum, Dad and eleven year old me are ready to drive to Sydney in the family's burgundy Mayflower, a car that looks like a child's drawing: boxy, squat, few rounded edges other than the mudguards. It is only one of four cars my parents ever own that isn't a Holden (the others being a small two-seater of no longer remembered manufacture that has a dickie seat and a canvas pull-down roof, a Mini Minor and a Corolla).

We set off in the evening, me in the back with blankets and a pillow. We drive out through Coburg and Fawkner, eventually getting onto the Hume Highway, still a two-lane blacktop. We make it safely over Pretty Sally, a hill I hear grown ups talking about with trepidation. 'Be careful going over Pretty Sally,' they say darkly. 'Dangerous bend there.'

At first I'm too excited to sleep, but somewhere along the road I nod off. When I wake up, we are a long way out of the city and Mum has taken over the driving. Everything is dark except for that part of the Hume lit up by the Mayflower's headlights and those of oncoming cars and trucks. The highway is littered with roadkill – rabbits, possums – and the trees ... the trees on both sides lean over the highway towards each other, almost meeting in the middle, where the white line separating the lanes runs. It is like waking up in a cavern, just like the one I now see on Kooyong Road, outside the palliative care hospice.

Several times when I come to visit Dad in Bethlehem I think about that trip, about the eucalyptus cave we drove through together in the Mayflower along the two lane blacktop dotted with dead animals.

⌣

The hospice foyer is dark. After a short wait there we follow as a nurse wheels him up to his ward.

⌣

Contrary to what has most often been his accommodation – a private, single bed room – Dad is wheeled into a small three-bed ward, a north-facing room with large windows; sunlight pours in through the trees. It is May, a beautiful autumn afternoon of the kind Melbourne does exceptionally well: balmy, sunny, the bluest of skies, a mid-afternoon hint of the crisp evening to come. Despite the cramped quarters and the company of two other elderly men – or, more likely, because of them – the room has a cheerful air to it.

'I am Jirí,' says the nearest man, his European accent strong. 'Hello.'

Jirí tells us that he came to Australia from Czechoslovakia. Czechoslovakia? At once, another sequence of memories is brought forth.

~

In the politically volatile year of 1968, Jack and I are living with our two children in Toronto. This is the year of the Martin Luther King Jnr and Robert Kennedy assassinations, the year when the war in Vietnam is ramped up several notches, when Lyndon B Johnson declares he will not stand nor will he accept the nomination to stand for president, when Tommie Smith and John Carlos, quietly supported by the third place winner Australian Peter Norman, raise their gloved fists in a Black Power salute from the winners' podium at the Mexico Olympic Games.

In Europe, the Paris uprising and general strike of millions of citizens occurs: 'Be realistic, demand the impossible' and 'What we want is everything.' So too does the Prague Spring, a moment of light and hope. Some weeks after Soviet troops crush the uprising, I receive an aerogram from Dad. He writes that he was a member of a delegation of peace workers, of Communist and Labor Party members, clergy and other Leftists, who travel to the Soviet embassy in Canberra to meet with the ambassador to protest the invasion. 'It was the most Difficult thing I ever had to do in my Political Life,' he writes.

When I receive this information, written in his flowing handwriting, my first smile is for his customary use of the old-fashioned Practice of capitalising the Important Nouns; sometimes, for particular emphasis, an Adjective. My second is for the significant news contained in his letter: 'I went as part of a Delegation to the Soviet Embassy to protest ...'

Remarkable, this.

'Dearest Dad,' I write. While I am astonished he has done this – his love of, belief in, the Soviet Union has never wavered – 'I know how difficult that must have been for you. All the more reason that I'm so moved that you took part. And proud.' It took courage, I tell him. I write a little more about life in Toronto, tell him about my continued work with refusers and resisters who come up over the border to escape being press-ganged into military service in the Vietnam War, enquire about what else is happening in his life, ask how's Mum, and sign off. 'Love, Sandra.'

Three weeks later, another aerogram. In this one, he expresses his Deep Regret. He says he was never more Sorry about anything he'd done in his Political Life. He wishes he'd never been part of that Delegation. 'NEVER.'

'Why?' I ask in a brief note (no chitchat this time). From the time I write the question to the time I receive his response, a little over four weeks pass. I take a paring knife from the kitchen drawer and slide open the aerogram's three glued flaps to read his reply.

It is the old story, the one about reactionary forces, pro-capitalist elements driving the protests, the CIA being behind it all. It was not, he writes, a people's uprising.

His letter makes me sad beyond measure.

Once or twice, after Jack and I permanently return to Australia, I try to talk with him about this incident, about our correspondence, but he entertains no more of it.

'That's enough,' he says on each occasion. 'No more. It's all over now.'
When he says 'It's all over now', to myself I hum 'baby blue'.

~

Two nurses, sweet-natured and kind, young and robust, help settle him while we, the only women in his life now (apart from the nursing staff), wait patiently in the corridor. His temperature, pulse rate, respiratory rate, oxygen level and blood pressure – his obs, as we learn to call them – are taken. Then, the nurse pokes her head out into the corridor and beckons us into the room.

Just as Dad is settling in against his pillows we hear a bird tweeting, very close by it seems. We turn to look in the direction of the sound.

'Bird,' Dad says in his whispery voice. 'Bird,' a little incredulous the second time. He smiles.

And there it is. In an elaborate white wire cage that hangs from a pole alongside the bed of Dad's yet-to-be-introduced roomie is a blue, white and grey budgerigar trilling its little lungs out.

We all smile. One of the nurses turns to us. 'Does he have a dog? A cat? A bird, perhaps? We welcome people's pets in here. It's nice for them to have their pets.' Touching. The nurse introduces us to the budgie – at least I think it's to the budgie. 'This is Charlie,' she says.

'G'day,' says the roomie whose bed the birdcage stands alongside. 'I'm Peter. This is me mate, Charlie.'

While Charlie continues to warble and Dad to smile, the nurse explains Bethlehem's procedures. Family may come in at any time of the day or night and stay as long as they want to. At the end of the corridor is a motel-style suite, equipped with several beds, a living room, a self-contained kitchen, and a full bathroom in which any or all of us may stay should we so desire. No charge. For their part, the hospice staff will keep Dad as comfortable as they possibly can.

Charlie heartens me, as does the room and its occupants. Why is it, then, that when a nurse offers a single room, I strenuously urge the others to accept? Habit? A result of him being in private wards most of those twenty-nine times? Do I agree, vehemence in every word, because I do not, not in these last days, want to share him with his roommates and their visitors, their families and friends? With their pets? To have to use up words on them, lose time in greetings and small talk?

Is it because I want him to myself?

My siblings and mother agree. And so it is that late on the second Bethlehem day Dad is moved into a dark, south-facing room with a splendid view of a brick wall. Sister Two and Sister Three nod when I suggest I draw the curtains; day and night, until he dies, they remain closed. The only light in the room emanates from a lamp on the bedside table.

~

Soon after being moved into the single room, his decline gathers speed. No point in food now. Meals brought to him on his first Bethlehem day, desserts for the most part, remain untouched. By day's end, the nursing staff stop delivering him food altogether.

Following the nurses' recommendation, Mum hires a special mattress, dark green with contours like a two dozen eggs tray. Placed on top of the standard mattress, it makes him more comfortable and less prone to bed sores, to back pain. He is hooked up to a saline drip laced with morphine that stands alongside the bedhead. On the other side is a bedside cupboard with four drawers. Each of the top two is half the width of the full-width drawers below them. One is the lock drawer where his drugs would have been kept were he still ingesting them; the other contains his shaving gear, toothpaste and a toothbrush. Below them are the drawers for his clothes, which, by now, consist only of the freshly washed pyjamas Mum brings him from home.

Two more days pass; they feel interminable. Sunny autumn days, chilly nights. I continue with my evening vigils, hours of sitting, sometimes topping up with a shorter early morning visit. Sometimes I talk to him, though by now he is comatose: 'Remember when …?', 'I was thinking about the time we …'. Most often, 'I love you, Dad.'

When a person is in a coma, it is understood that the last of their senses to go is hearing. Does he hear me reminisce, hear me say 'I love you?'

~

I sit in a chair next to his bed (I contemplate lying down alongside him, but the bed is too narrow to take both of us), hold his papery hand, and stroke, stroke, stroke it. I touch his face, this man who had made me, who I struggled with, fought with, loved and hated. I kissed him and stroked, too, his bald head, beautifully round and still freckled after all these years.

Don't go, Dad. Don't go. Not yet. Please.

~

On the fourth night, as I sit alongside him, he suddenly cries out. His voice is more resonant than it has been in months; it's almost strong. 'Sandra,' he commands, 'I want you to do it. Come on, Sandra, do it. Now, please.'

I jump up out of the chair. Even though I say 'Do what, Dad?' I know what he wants.

'Do it, please.' Now he is begging.

'I can't, Dad, I …'

'Please.'

Shaking uncontrollably, I look around the room, frantic, hoping to see someone who might save me. No one here. Just me. Me and Dad. I rattle the drawers of the bedside cabinet. 'Dad, I can't. They've locked the drawers. I can't get anything out of here.' I know there are no drugs in there, so why would it matter that the drawer is locked? I'll never know the answer to that, though I presume it's usual practice, drugs or no drugs.

Yes, he has been a member of the Voluntary Euthanasia Society of Victoria for years. Yes, he wanted to choose the where (at home) and the when (when he says he is ready) and the how (palliative doses of morphine) of his death. It is not to be. During the course of his twenty-ninth admission, it becomes clear his wishes will not be met.

～

Just before his admission to Bethlehem, Dad summons Ezra, his pharmacist friend, comrade and peace movement colleague of long standing. When Ezra arrives, Dad shoos everyone else out of the room and has the last one out close the door as they leave. Fifteen minutes later, Ezra, tall, square-jawed, handsome, emerges from the room; he is crying. Through his tears

Ezra tells those of us waiting in the hall that Dad has pleaded with him to get hold of something, anything, that would enable him to die. Ezra, long since retired, tells Dad he no longer has access to drugs and, even if he did, he doesn't have it in him to help Dad to die.

There are many possible explanations why Ezra does not help Dad. Perhaps he is disturbed by the suddenness of Dad's request. Perhaps, even though he is not observant, he feels obliged to conform with Talmudic law, which forbids suicide, assisted or self-generated. Perhaps he does not want to go against the law of the land, no matter how much he disagrees with it politically. Most likely, Ezra just doesn't want to – can't – do it.

~

'Please, *please.*' He is a child, begging for one more lolly. 'Please, Sandra. Sandy, please. Darling.'

We are holding on to each other. He cups my face in his hand; one finger idly flickers back and forth, a windscreen wiper on my cheek, surprising me because I think he has not been conscious enough to realise I am crying or that we are having this conversation. Even so, he seems not to see me; his eyes are half closed and not at all focused. 'Please do it. Do it for me.'

'Dad …' I say, sobbing.

'Do it, Sandra.' Now his voice is commanding, unwavering. 'Do it the way the Japanese did it.'

Stunned, I recoil from him. As I leap back, I knock over the chair. It lands on the lino with a thunderous clatter. 'What? What do you mean?'

'You know, the Japanese …' His voice trails off.

Does he want me to hack off his head? Surely not. A mad moment passes in which David Bowie and Ryuichi Sakamoto appear before me. 'Merry Christmas, Mr Lawrence,' I whisper and gulp down a giggle.

'Dad?'

'Please, Sandra, darling Sandy, do it for me.'

Darling Sandy, do it for me. You bastard. You old *bastard*.

Does he know what he is saying? Can he hear how loudly I weep? Does he see how many tissues I yank out of the box on his bedside table? What does he feel knowing that I, his oldest daughter, won't help him to die? Does he feel betrayed? Disappointed? Is he conscious enough to feel anything?

Childish thoughts – or are they thoughts of childhood? – scurry through my mind like rats in a roof. Uppermost of these thoughts: will he be angry with me? Disapprove of me? Most ludicrous of all: will he punish me?

The moment – if that's all it was, and I had then and still now, more than twenty years later, no notion at all of just how long this incident takes – the moment passes and he settles down again, his breathing, while even, a little shallower than it was this morning.

Does he believe that I, like Ezra, have let him down? Is his quiet, simple resignation his acceptance that he is going to have to live out what's left of his life?

We hold hands. With my free hand, I pat the top of his right, which is holding mine with surprising strength. After a while, his grip begins to loosen, until he lets go altogether and both his hands flop onto the blue thermal cotton blanket.

A nurse pops her head in the doorway. Cheerful as ever, she says, 'Everything alright in here, Sandra?'

Did she hear me crying? Did she hear Dad begging for an end? Yelling about the Japanese? Pleading with me to … what?

If she did, she says nothing about it.

I nod and, just as quietly as she appeared, she walks off down the corridor.

~

Not yet ready to return to my apartment, unable to bear the pain of this episode alone, I drive to Mum's, where I find my sisters sitting with Mum at the living-room table. They are drinking tea and playing Scrabble, as much an arena of fierce competitive battle between us as a game played for pleasure.

'You're not making *another* seven letter word, are you?'

'That's not how you spell …'

'Yes, it is.'

'Get the dictionary.'

As I enter, they all look up from the board to me, expectant. Mum has an affectionate half-smile on her face. 'How is he?' she asks.

Sister Two is more observant. 'What's wrong?' she says. She pulls the chestnut braid that hangs between her narrow shoulders to the front and begins to tug at the end of it.

After I recount what happened, I finish with: 'He has the death rattles. It won't be long now.'

Two stands up to hug me. 'Poor San,' she says, using her name of deepest affection for me. Tall and lean, Sister Two wraps me in her willowy arms and holds me tight while I sob into her green mohair cardigan. 'How awful.'

'What did you do?' says Sister Three, who remains seated.

I tell them what I did, how terrified I felt that the drawer might be unlocked, even though I knew his drugs drawer never is and even if it had been there are no drugs in it anyway.

'Darling,' Mum says in her most tender voice. 'Here, sit. Do you want some tea? A piece of fruit?' In times past, in a crisis – there have been several – she would offer whiskey, but it is ten years since I've been a drinker.

'Whiskey, please. I'll get it.'

'No,' she says without so much as a raised eyebrow, 'let me.'

She gets up from her chair and shuffles to the buffet, on top of which she keeps some bottles of booze, a cut-crystal decanter and glasses – whiskey tumblers, stemmed wine glasses, another type of glass for vermouth. The overhead light makes the decanter sparkle and flash – blue, purple, red, yellow, green lights: an Aurora Borealis emanating from Mum's 1950s Danish teak buffet.

'Poor darling,' Mum says, handing me the drink with one hand, patting my cheek with the other. She holds the whiskey decanter slightly aloft towards Two.

'You bet,' says Two.

'Not for me,' says Three.

Mum pours for Sister Two and herself, plonks the decanter on the table, sits down and raises her glass low in the air.

'L'chaim.' In Yiddish, she toasts to life.

'L'chaim.' I take a large gulp and sigh as the tawny liquid slithers like a lava flow down my throat and into my belly. Ah yes, I remember this.

While they fuss over me, we all shed another round of tears. So many tears. Awash with weeping.

After an hour, I say my goodbyes and go home. Exhausted though I am, I run a bath. Even before it is filled, I climb in, more than ready for a good, long soak. Lulled by the warmth, I soon fall asleep. By the time I wake, the water has turned stone cold, my skin is purple and wrinkled, and I am shivering. I have not one microgram of energy left. I clamber out of the bath, stumble the few steps to my bedroom without drying off, flop on the bed, wrap myself in the doona, and before the count of five fall into a deep, dreamless sleep.

~

The next day, Sister Two and I go together to Bethlehem in the late morning. Dad is tossing about in his bed, moaning so loudly he can be heard the length of the corridor. Is he in pain? Is he battling his demons? Have the Japanese got him? Two and I hasten our steps.

He seems not to realise we are there.

A nurse comes by. 'I think he needs some pain medication,' she says. 'What if I get him some morphine?'

We look at each other, at the nurse, and nod, first to each other, then to the nurse.

'Yes,' we say in unison. Sister Two pleads, 'Please give him something.'

The nurse goes off down the hallway; within minutes she is back, carrying a hypodermic syringe in a plastic kidney tray. She is poised to go when Dad surprises us by yelling – well, really, it was another form of the moaning – 'No, no, no.'

'There, there, Mr G,' the nurse says in her best professional voice. 'It's alright. It won't hurt.'

As vigorously as he is able, Dad shakes his head from side to side. 'No. Don't … don't want …'

For all his years, all his medical and dental treatments, he never overcomes his fear of injections, yet it is my strong feeling that his protestation on this occasion isn't about his fear of the needle or even about pain. It's something else. But what? Two and I step into the hallway and peer back in through the doorway, watching, leaving the nurse to do her dirty work – to do *our* dirty work. In the year after Dad dies, Two and I speak of and correspond about this incident several times, both regretting that we allowed it to occur. We agree that, although we were never sure what the signs were, we misread them, badly; whatever his reason for not wanting the shot, it was most likely not about his fear of the discomfort of an injection. Two believes that, having been unable to get any assistance to die quietly on his own terms in his own home, he just wanted to see out the process as it unfolded, pain and all.

Is she right? I'm not so sure, but we will never know.

When I return to Bethlehem later that night, all is quiet. A peaceful, uneventful hour passes before I bid him goodnight, and then leave for home.

∿

The following night, Mum is still in the room when I arrive. We step into the hall for a quick chat before she leaves for home and dinner with Two and Three.

'Will you drop in to watch the doco on your way home?' Mum is referring to an SBS documentary, a tenth anniversary look back at the Vietnam Moratorium Campaign to be screened at ten. As much as

Mum wants to see the documentary, she wants more to have all her daughters around her, together, as often as possible. Watching this documentary on television presents one such opportunity.

～

It has been many years since Sisters Two and Three have lived in Victoria, Three for the longest time. Distance in particular means that High Holy day gatherings no longer occur too often. Moreover, as Mum grows old, the less able she is to find relief from the constant pain that beleaguers her, the more exhausted she becomes, the events of the Jewish calendar – Pesach, Rosh Hashanah, Yom Kippur – become too much for her to manage. She is no longer able to cook for the twenty to thirty family members she once prepared for – daughters and their husbands or partners, grandchildren, inlaws, nieces and nephews – and she is too proud – too damn stubborn – to ask for help. Even when help is offered, she turns it down. 'It's alright, thanks, dear. I'll be fine.'

～

Mum wants us to watch the documentary together, hoping to catch a glimpse of her husband at the head of the throng.

'I'll see how I feel,' I reply.

She shakes her head and walks slowly down the hall. It is clear from her gait that her degenerating spine, her arthritic hips, are troubling her more than usual tonight. I watch until she disappears into the lift, then turn and enter the room.

～

His lips are swollen dry, so I take a large cotton bud, moisten it in the glass of water on his bedside table and dab it on his lips. Unlike on other occasions, when he manages to express his gratitude in one way or another – a nod, a slight squeeze of my hand, a tap of his forefinger on the bedclothes – this time he is unable to respond.

Just as I finish dabbing the water – first on his bottom lip, then his upper – and am about to sit down, he begins to cough and splutter. Oh fuck, he's choking. Some of the water from the cotton bud must have dribbled the wrong way down his throat. Oh my god. Frantic, I look around for something to ease his choking, but can't see a thing. I don't even know what it is I am supposed to be looking for. All of a sudden, when I'm about to run out the door to find a nurse (why do I forget to use the bedside buzzer to call?), he stops and settles himself.

In my panic, my own throat has become dry. I sit on the chair, sip from the glass of water and clear my throat. Unexpectedly, I find myself singing. Humming, more like it, the plaintive notes of a Paul Robeson song. '*Oh my baby, my curly-headed baby …*'

~

Once upon a time I had a voice. I sang in coffee lounges, occasionally at folk music concerts, at communist youth league camps. On one occasion, I was part of the entertainment on the RHMS Ellinis, *the ship I travelled on to London in 1964. I sang on ban the bomb marches. A Joan Baez devotee – I grew my hair long and ironed it straight – I sang Australian, British and American folk songs, antiwar and union songs: 'Study War No More' and 'Joe Hill', 'Donna Donna', 'Down in the Valley', 'Irene, Goodnight', 'Black Is the Colour …', melancholy – some might say mournful – tunes that appeal to that side of my temperament. On top of a bookcase in my office, which doubles as a guestroom, there is a photo of me sitting in a gutter during a 1962 Frankston to Melbourne ban the bomb march, accompanying myself on guitar, which I taught myself to play.*

I'm gonna lay down my sword and shield
Down by the riverside …
Ain't gonna study war no more
Study war no more …

In this photo, I'm wearing a dark grey jumper, a grey Mum calls anthracite. The jumper – Shetland wool as I recall, which I borrow from Mum's wardrobe for the occasion and never return – has a rollneck. My hair is pinned up in a French roll; strands of hair have escaped from the bobby pins that are holding the roll in place as best they can. I am nineteen and gorgeous, sitting there on the kerb of the Nepean Highway in Cheltenham, where we, teenage Youth Peace Group activists and old-hand Victorian Peace Committee demonstrators against French atomic testing in the Pacific and the American incursion in Vietnam, have stopped for a rest on our two-day march from Frankston to the State Library. We march in solidarity with and in imitation of Britain's Campaign for Nuclear Disarmament marchers: Frankston to Melbourne is a similar distance to that marched by the British demonstrators, who walked from Aldermaston to London.

~

Here I am now, more than thirty-five years later, still holding a tune, if somewhat breathily after decades of cigarette smoking. '*Oh my baby, my curly-headed baby …*'

By the second line I realise I have started too high, that the higher notes are difficult to reach – no, they are unreachable – so I drop down an octave or two. Or three.

Paul Robeson. This is his song. Everyone in our family loves it. Even before we meet him, we love him. Hero of the people. Robeson's records take pride of place in our family's catholic collection.

'Hey, everyone,' Dad says one night when he comes home from a meeting of the peace committee, 'guess who's coming to dinner?'

Today's announcement is about the man himself, Paul Robeson.

Rendered speechless, my sisters and I gasp.

~

Dad gives me Howard Fast's *Peekskill USA* to read. It is one of many books of the politically progressive canon he has me read to advance my political education. I am to recount what I have learnt from this book at my Sunday morning read and report sessions. After he dies, I take the book from his shelves and make it my own. As I hold it in my hand, I realise the extent to which I have imagined the shape, the texture, the beauty of this book.

For years, in my mind's eye, whenever I think about this slender volume, it has the ragged-cut pages of thick cream-coloured paper one comes across only in American books. It is beautifully bound in matching cream board with a burgundy leather spine; the lettering on the front cover is gold. All that is real about this memory – this fantasy? – is the cream board of the cover. True, the spine is burgundy, but it is fabric, not leather. The title and author text are also burgundy, somewhat darker than Soviet red; it is not gold.

And what of the inside? Following the black and white photo of a smiling Robeson standing at a microphone, surrounded by bodyguards, some of whom appear to be wearing military uniform – navy, army – the title page reveals the discrepancy between my memory and reality. Near the bottom, these words: *Foreign Languages Publishing House, Moscow, 1954.*

There follows in Cyrillic type what I presume to be a preface, then another in English, and then the text of Fast's recounting.

The pages are classic Foreign Languages Publishing, of which I have seen many volumes. Not ragged cut, not at all thick, the paper, now browned with age (and, quite likely, cigarette smoke) is flimsy, the lines of type too close, the typeface just that little bit too fine.

∽

Peekskill recounts a 1949 civil rights fundraiser to be held in the upstate New York town of Peekskill, where Robeson, Pete Seeger (another guess who's coming to dinner announcement) and others are to perform. At Peekskill, whose population is notoriously conservative and where an active branch of the Ku Klux Klan is known to exist, a white mob attacks the performers and the audience – most of them African Americans and Jews – who are there to enjoy the concert. Author Howard Fast is there to help set up. The Klan mob breaks the seating, smashes sound equipment and burns song sheets. Police, who offer no support to the Leftists, declare the concert over.

The concert is rescheduled for the following weekend. More than twenty thousand people show up, as does an angry racist crowd, who scream 'Go back to Russia' and 'Jew, Jew, Jew' and 'Dirty stinkin' Yid', some of which epithets I am accustomed to have slung at me, especially – though not only – at school: 'Go back to Russia, ya commie' and 'Ya dirty Jew. Ya kike.'

Over the top of the harassment, Robeson sings on.

I dreamed I saw Joe Hill last night
Alive as you and me
Says I, 'But Joe you're ten years dead.'
'I never died,' says he …

Even as a child, I know he is one of us, a Leftist, a democrat. Bubbeh takes me more than once, more than twice, to see *Show Boat*.

～

New York City, 1993. Uptown in Harlem, the Studio Museum has an exhibit I am keen to see. From Union Square station, I take the subway north. At the West 125th Street stop, I alight, go up the stairs and walk towards the museum. Two doors before I reach my destination, I look up and notice a sign, which juts out onto the street. In black type on white background, it reads: Paul Robeson Family Medical Center.

It's been years since I've thought about Robeson. Now, seeing his name up there makes me smile. I want to spin around, to shout and point: 'Hey, I met him. He came to my house.' I remain silent, a grinning white woman with a secret knowledge, standing on the pavement in Harlem in front of a community medical centre on West 125th.

~

Thinking about Robeson as I sit there alongside Dad's bed, as I sing, I see Robeson in my mind's eye, standing tall at the front of the riverboat, standing tall in front of our fireplace, his anthropologist, activist wife Eslanda – Essie – alongside him.

Meeting luminaries such as Robeson was, it could be said, one of the perks of having a dad who was the state secretary of the Campaign for International Cooperation and Disarmament.

It is impossible to tell if Dad can hear me and, if he can, whether my singing irritates or soothes him. Words I can't remember, I hum over. I just keep rollin' along.

And so I go, singing and humming my way through songs popularised by Robeson until I can think of no more. Then I switch to Tin Pan Alley: 'Sunny Side of the Street', 'Red, Red Robin', 'Jeepers, Creepers', 'Bicycle Built for Two'. *Daisy, Daisy, give me your answer, do …*

~

My daughter is pregnant with her first child. I meet her and her husband at the front bar of Pellegrini's in Bourke Street, where generations of my family have been patrons since the Pellegrini brothers first opened their doors in 1954.

The parents to be have been to-ing and fro-ing about the baby's name: my daughter favours Daisy for a girl, her husband does not. Daisy is a name I also like. As I approach where they sit at the end of the bar near the espresso machine, I lean into my son-in-law and quietly sing in his ear: 'Daisy, Daisy, give me your answer, do …' I expect him to laugh, or to give his characteristic chuckle, which is more like a grunt and an exhalation of air through his nose, but instead he glares at me. Not directly, but in the mirror that lines the wall behind the bar.

As it happens, the baby is a boy, who they name Milo, after a character in Catch-22.

~

I sing slowly, quietly, smiling all the while, gently tapping out a rhythm with my foot on the polished linoleum. Pete Seeger next, then some of the Russian songs Bubbeh taught me – 'Ochi Chiornye', though these two words are all I remember of this song, so I hum or *ta dum* the rest, and, in English, 'Song of the Volga Boatmen'. By the time I arrive at Mac.Robertsons Girls' High, where we students learn to sing this song, I have already been singing it for years. Then comes 'Kalinka', a song on a 33⅓ recording of the Red Army Choir ('Do you know of any other army in the world, Sandra, that would have its own choir?'). Bold red type – of course – on a black background.

Ka ling, kaka ling
Kaka ling commeye ya …

Until I begin to write this book, that's how I understand the word breaks, how I sing them. When I check the transliterated spelling, I learn the correct phrasing. It's all in the timing (what isn't?).

Kalinka, kalinka
Kalinka moya …

Inexplicably, surprisingly, I soon realise I am singing Hatikvah, Israel's national anthem, the melancholy of which is irresistible to me. Even though I am able to sing only its first five lines, I do not understand at all what they mean. The only Hebrew words I know are *Shabbat shalom* (Sabbath peace), *toda* (thank you), *layla tov* (goodnight), *Shana Tova* (have a good year) and *Shalom aleykhim* (peace be with you). Not in 4/4 time and one of the least militaristic of the world's national anthems – an irony that has never escaped me – HaTikvah always puts me in mind of Smetena's *The Moldau*. Not surprisingly, it seems: late in my life, I take the trouble to learn that the song's melody comes directly from Smetena.

> *Kol od balevave*
> *P'nimah*
> *Nefesh Yehudi homiyah*
> *Ulfa'atey mizrach kadimah*
> *Ayin l'tzion tzofiyah.*

~

Traditional Jews is what we are. Sister Three has long since become an observant Buddhist; Sister Two has little interest in being Jewish or, as far as I know, in being Buddhist. Our parents haven't kept Shabbos since 1959, the year Bubbeh dies: no candles, no challah on the table on Friday night, though in our own secular way we continue to celebrate Pesach, Rosh Hashanah and Yom Kippur.

We keep some of the traditions of Pesach: the bitter herbs, the raw horseradish that reminds us of the bitter days of bondage under the Egyptian yoke and, in our household, reminds us of bondage everywhere, all curtailment of liberty. We eat matzot.

Dad loves matza pancakes, matza brei. *Not that he ever cooks one; Mum makes them for him.*

'Here, Sandra,' he says. While I wait for Mum to cook one for me, he pushes his plate towards me: 'Have a bite. Delicious.'

Most breakfasts for the eight days of Pesach, the same.

At Rosh Hashanah, apple and honey to portend a sweet year.

A socialist since his teens, Dad is often heard at holiday times muttering about religion being the opiate of the masses. On a rare occasion, he tells one of his favourite stories, about how, when he is fourteen and at his father's funeral, the rabbi slaps his face because he doesn't cry over his father's death – at least not in the rabbi's presence.

'Boy, your father just died. Why aren't you weeping? You are a shameful son,' the rabbi, who bar mitzvahed him only a year before, admonishes.

'I never – never – went to shul again.' Dad always finishes off with a flourish of smug satisfaction. That'll show 'em, the story seems to say, although I do come to wonder, as I come to wonder about many of his stories, if this is another expression of the bravado he employs to hide his deep pain. Whenever he tells the story about being slapped in the face by the rabbi, he is always angry and, I come to feel in later years, rather sad.

Except for a wedding, a death, a bat or bar mitzvah, he never goes to shul. Even then, he goes, he says, only because Mum makes him.

⁓

I put aside the few words I know of HaTikvah but continue to hum the melody. Or is it *The Moldau* I'm humming?

⁓

One night, after a long sit with Dad and, later, a soak in the bath, I go to bed at around ten o'clock, at least three hours earlier than usual. Asleep, I dream.

My bath is filled with loosely set raspberry jelly. When I step out onto the bathmat, wobbly lumps of red jelly slip off my arms and legs and torso onto the mat. I shake off the remaining globs of jelly, dry off, get dressed and leave my apartment.

When I wake, I am laughing. Was that a born-again dream?

~

My favourite Italian song appears on a 12-inch LP of popular Italian songs Mum buys in the 1950s. 'La Montanara', 'Song of the Mountains', has a stirring melody, but because I remember only the two words of its title, this one I hum. 'La Montanara' is a song beloved by partisans fighting the fascists in the mountains where they hide and live.

Being now in Italy with my singing, I arrive at a lively revolutionary song, 'Avanti Popolo (Bandiera Rossa)'. 'Bandiera Rossa' is one of many songs sung by thousands of people, of whom I am one, who march in Melbourne and cities around the world on May Day. '*Stai indossando la tua bandiera rossa?*' my Italian neighbour asks if I show up at her North Fitzroy shop in a less than jovial mood. 'Have you got your red rag on?' She cackles at her own joke. 'The Red Flag' completes my trio of Italian revolutionary and workers' songs. Of course there is also 'Bella Ciao', which I sing slowly, my voice soft. These are followed by songs from the Spanish Civil War, 'Viva la Quince Brigada', 'Freiheit' and 'The Four Insurgent Generals'. How deep down in memory these songs have been stored, yet tonight they readily resurface.

A gentle Aboriginal song and a Japanese lullaby, both from my schooldays. As I sing the opening line of the latter – '*Sakura, sakura …*' – I wonder how it comes to be that so soon after the end of the Second World War, when anti-Japanese feeling still runs deep and wide in the Australian community, schoolchildren are taught this song.

What about the folk songs from *Reedy River*, Dick Diamond's musical play about the 1891 shearers' strike, performed in 1959 by New Theatre? In 1961, I have a short turn on the boards with New Theatre, performing in its production of *The Good Soldier Schweik*.

Songs by Billie Holiday, Glen Miller tunes – I dredge up everything I can think of. The sweet second movement melody of Beethoven's seventh.

⁓

Mum says that in the years Dad comes courting, he carries with him what today would be called a box set, something similar to a large photo album, that contains five double-sided shellac 78 RPM recordings of Beethoven's Symphony No. 7 in A Major. *It is the most precious thing he owns. His love of Beethoven lasts all his life.*

⁓

It crosses my mind to sing the opening of Beethoven's fifth, the first record I ever owned, a present for my sixteenth birthday, but I feel that even softly humming it would be too insistent, too adamant, so I leave it alone. (The first record I buy with my own money, earned working a school holidays job at Myer, is a Snooks Eaglin album; the second is Bill Haley and His Comets' *Rock Around the Clock*.)

Singing, singing, singing ... What am I really doing, singing these songs to him? Am I re-creating my youth, staving off my own old age, my own death? Am I reliving my life, with him, with my family, with friends and comrades through song? Is that what I am doing?

~

For years after Dad dies, Mum will say, two or three times a year, 'I often think about you sitting beside him, singing. You know, don't you, he probably heard you, even if he was unconscious?'

~

The low-wattage globe gives off a light as soft as my singing. For the first time since Dad is moved to Bethlehem – six days now – the room feels comfortable, just right: a Goldilocks room. I flick off my shoes, resettle myself in the chair and continue to sing songs from around the world that our family listened to on vinyl records decades before the term 'world music' becomes a glimmer in record company executives' eyes. Charles Trenet; Edith Piaf ('*La Mer*', I sing, '*Je ne regret rien*', even if that isn't true – for him or for me; surely not for Piaf either), the castanets, guitars and flamenco-heeled shoes of José Greco and his company of dancers; Israeli songs, Greek songs, folk songs and blues from America and England, 'Blowin' in the Wind', 'We Shall Overcome' and Buddy Holly's 'Everyday', one of the few pop songs he ever enjoys.

~

'Turn that damned racket down! Bloody rock'n'roll. Bloody American crap.'

'Everyday' as rock'n'roll? Sweet enough, but definitely not rock, not to me.

His daughters, disappointed at not being allowed to listen to Stan 'The Man' Rofe on 3KZ, giggle at his swearing.

~

Eureka Youth League songs, stirring songs about striking miners, Irish rebel Kevin Barry, Australian bushranger heroes – Bold Jack Donohue, Ben Hall, the Wild Colonial Boy.

And 'The Internationale'. Of course, 'The Internationale'.

Arise ye workers from your slumber
Arise ye prisoners of want ...

There will be no more arising from his slumber for this worker, whose days of want have long since passed. Long since.

~

After the war is over, his service completed, he would have liked to go to university to study law. Quite likely, he would have made a good lawyer, persuasively argumentative as he is. But there are already two children, so a living has to be earned. No university for this returned soldier. No, a job must be found.

Melbourne's Flinders Lane is the centre of the clothing trade before and during the war and for many years after. Here, for a time, he finds work – most memorably, in a factory that manufactures sequins. Sometimes he brings home little cellophane packets of sequins, each containing a different colour. Are they given to him? Does he nick them? These thoughts never occur to me when I am a child. All that matters then is that they are bright, they sparkle; the metal ones are the brightest. The ones made of a sticky jelly-like texture are translucent. There is a time when no matter where in our house you cast your eyes, they will likely land on a sequin or two.

How long does he work at the sequin factory? I don't know, but certainly for as long as we live in the Alma Road flat in East St Kilda. Possibly longer still, because I have memories of sequins in the carpet at Wavenhoe Avenue, the house that backs onto Alma Road opposite the St Kilda Cemetery gate, though it's also possible that Mum brought the little sequin packets with us when we moved.

~

The volume of his rattling breath increases, becomes more laboured. I sing on. Hum on. Beethoven, Mozart, Ellington, more, more and more still: a phrase here, whole lines there, whole songs, whole melodies. Just when my memory seems depleted, I return again and again to Robeson. In my bones I know Dad won't mind the repetition.

Deep river, my home is over Jordan …

A quarter to ten rolls around. Three hours of singing have passed. Exhaustion overwhelms me. My mouth is dry, my bones are aching, my lips are chapped. I reach for the glass of water on the bedside table and sip from it. Did water ever taste so sweet?

Dad's lips, too, are dry, so once again I douse an oversized cotton bud into what remains of the water and dab it along his lips, more carefully this time. He does not stir.

Sitting there in Dad's room, which I've come to call 'Dad's cupboard', in the chair I take as close to his bed as is possible, I pause in my singing and listen. The only sound is his rattling breath. Then, for just a moment as she passes his room, the sound of the efficient *pit pat pit pat pit pat* of a nurse's footsteps on the polished linoleum floor. Within seconds the footfall fades, and then is gone.

His breath rattles way down in his chest. A death rattle. Some part of my mind acknowledges this is it, this is the night he will die. Another part ignores it. Represses it. Denies it. *Not yet, Dad, not yet, Daddy. Stay a while longer.*

I toss the used cotton bud into the wastepaper basket and stand. Overwhelmed, depleted, I feel I must leave, even if just for a while. Go home. Have a shower, a little lie down, change into fresh clothes. So I pick up my purse, wrap my fringed woollen scarf around my neck, whisper 'Goodnight, Dad. Back soon', leave the room and drive very slowly to Mum's house.

~

There they are, the other three women of our family, seated around the dining table watching the television, the Scrabble board in the middle with only three or four moves on it. As I enter, they all turn away from the television to look at me, wave hello, and then look back to the screen. My attention also turns to the screen. Together we watch napalm rain down on a Vietnamese hamlet. Vietnamese women and children, elderly men, all running, trying to escape the mayhem, the deadly flames. Watching the thatched huts going up in flames, seeing the screaming, seeing the fear, all the images and sounds emanating from the screen in Mum's well-ordered living room almost twenty-five years after the war has ended ...

~

One warm, midsummer night, two years earlier, at about nine o'clock, I am seated at my dining-room table reading the newspaper. My ears prick up at the sound of the approaching thwop thwop thwop *of a helicopter. In a matter of minutes it is hovering overhead, right over my garden it seems, its spotlight on high beam. In what appears to be a tight circle, it swoops over one backyard after another, illuminating all the neighbouring houses as it goes. The noise is terrifying.*

What would it be like, I wonder that night, as I wonder in the 1960s and 1970s when I watch the war on the news, to live with that incessant thunder of helicopters, B-52s, bomb and napalm drops blasting their way through every single day, every single night? It is impossible to imagine. Even though the helicopter is hovering over my back garden, as noisy as it is, it provides barely a glimpse.

~

As the thatched roof blazes, I move my gaze from the screen to look at Mum, at my sisters.

'Well?' Mum smiles up at me, softly.

It is odd that she asks. She must have heard his rattling when she was with him earlier, before she left that evening.

228

'How is he?' Sister Three asks, her eyes darting from me to the screen and back again. I look hard at my youngest sister, at her steel-grey curls, her dark brown eyes, her freckles. Handsome, I think. A handsome woman.

'Hello, Sandra,' says Sister Two.

'Hello, Two.'

I slump into a chair, his chair, at the head of the table. Although the table is a perfect square, it is where he sits, so that is the head. As I sit down, Sister Two stands, moves to the sideboard, lifts the crystal decanter into the air and, raising her eyebrows, asks the question.

'Thanks,' I say. I stare at the Scandinavian sideboard. Despite the intervening years, nothing about it seems any less modern than when Mum buys it in the 1950s. It's likely I think so because the sideboard and I age together, alongside each other as it were, so it, like me, doesn't seem to be at all out of fashion. It doesn't seem to have aged.

Two pours a stiff shot into one of the whiskey tumblers and places it on the table in front of me. There it sits, untouched.

'I think the end is close,' I say to them.

Onscreen, B-52s scream. Mouths agape, the villagers of – which of so many villages is it? – scream too, though their screams are inaudible. The B-52s obliterate their cries, just as they burn and obliterate their homes, burn and obliterate their fields, burn and obliterate their neighbours. The flames burn their skin, their hair. But the gaping mouths, their wide-stretched eyes – you don't have to hear to know they are screaming, to see how much pain they are in, how terrified they are. They run. Half naked, fully naked, their clothes burnt off, they run. Running running running running …

Mum nods, a slow nod; she is no longer smiling. Two says, 'Oh.' Three remains silent.

'He has …' I hesitate. 'His breath is …' Again, hesitation. 'His breathing is laboured. It won't be long now.'

BOOM! A thatched-roofed hut explodes upwards into tiny, flaming fragments that fall, like fireflies, from high in the air back to the ground.

We look at each other, down at our laps, back to each other. Some glances at the television screen. The words 'It won't be long now' hover.

And then, the strangest thing happens, though it has to be said it didn't seem strange at the time. The strangeness of it occurs to me only years later.

What happens is this: all four of us settle in our chairs and, without a word, continue to sip tea or whiskey, to watch the television, while we wait for him, the vibrant living him, to appear on the screen.

In the years since Dad's death, I have thought often about that night. Why did I leave him? Why, after I'd had a drink with Mum, didn't I go back to Bethlehem to be with him? And not only do I wonder. I have mercilessly lacerated myself: why did you let him die alone? Why didn't you go to the public phone at the hospice and call Mum to tell her and the sisters to come so we could all be with him? Because, even though I leave Bethlehem believing I am taking a break for only an hour or so, that I will soon return, that he will wait for me to come back, I must have known. Really, I must have.

Don't I say when I arrived at Mum's, 'It won't be long now'?

I do. That's what I say. Yet here we sit. Here *I* sit.

More images of the war fill the screen, then, before too long, the footage turns to the moratorium and the march from Treasury Gardens into the city along Bourke Street.

'There he is!' Mum exclaims, pointing to the screen.

Yes, there he is, in the middle of the lead line, arms linked with Jim Cairns on one side, Jean McLean of Save Our Sons on the other.

'Look at those sideburns,' says Sister Two.

We chuckle at the unsightly mutton chops, furry creatures that cling to the sides of his face. Electrical Trades Union state secretary Ted Innes sports the same sideburns, but even though Ted is a chunkier man, his hair darker, denser, his complexion ruddier, his sideburns look just as silly as Dad's.

'And the specs,' says Three.

In the 1970s, Dad wears heavy black-framed glasses. Fashionable though they might have been, they never did suit the fine bone structure of his face.

Me, Two and Three, Mum, we watch the documentary. By film's end I am twitching from exhaustion. 'I'm going home for a scrub up and a bit of a nap,' I tell them. Half an hour or so, I say, then I'll go back to the hospice. 'See you there.'

~

Squawking of my front-door buzzer wakes me. It's nearly three o'clock in the morning. I have been sleeping since around eleven-thirty. As I struggle to wake up, to get out of bed, my limbs feel leaden, my head thick. 'Who is it?' I ask into the intercom, as if I didn't know.

'It's me,' Sister Two announces herself. At once, I am furious with myself and racked with guilt. Why didn't I just go back to the hospice?

Here it is again, the same question as earlier: why didn't I ring the others from Bethlehem and suggest they come there, soon? Why did we stay watching the television?

Two comes up the stairs to my apartment, a spacious late 1950s, first-floor one-bedroom that has, from the kitchen window, a thin slice of a view of Port Phillip Bay, visible through a gap between two low-rise apartment blocks. She tells me that Dad died a bit after two o'clock. When the hospice phones to tell Mum that he's died, they assure her that two nurses are with him when he 'passed away', an expression none of us approve of.

Do they say so to reassure Mum that he hasn't died alone? Do the staff sense Mum's guilt because she isn't there in the moment? Perhaps they understand this form of guilt. Can they even begin to imagine Mum's terror of being alone when she dies, her horror of leaving anyone she loves on their own when they are dying? I have often wondered if saying 'We were with your loved one when they passed away; they weren't alone' is what palliative carers and nurses in hospitals and hospices are trained to say to alleviate family members' guilt, their sorrow, their shame, perhaps, at not having been there in the moment of death. Even if that were true, it never relieved me of mine.

～

Sister Two waits while I dress; we talk quietly. No tears, not yet. When I am ready, we go downstairs and walk slowly along the garden path to the street. The damp early morning air smells of salty dew and seaweed. We drive off in her car, heading towards Glen Eira Road.

We have just passed Ripponlea Station when we hear the whine of a police siren. Sister Two looks in the rear-view mirror. 'Fucking hell,' she says. 'Stay here. Keep quiet.'

It is a good thing that she, more able than me to remain calm in the face of stupidity, is the one who gets out of the car to speak with the two men who get out of theirs. Inside her car, I have already begun to fume.

Two police, younger than either of our sons by a good ten years, saunter up to Two, peer inside the car and see me. 'What are we doing out so late at night, ladies?'

Crime number 2: asking why two adult women old enough to be their grandmothers might be out in the wee hours. Crime number 1? A double: referring to us as ladies and using the plural personal pronoun. Two calmly explains that our Dad has just died and we are on our way to our mother's house, which is just up the road. Unrelenting – and indifferent – they continue with their questions. Because I know her well, I can tell that after ten or so minutes (it could have been less), Two is becoming agitated.

When they feel they have fulfilled their civic duty, they let us go with a caution to take it easy on the road. We drive off in our direction, they in theirs.

'Fucking idiots.' Which of the two of us says that? Possibly, in a moment of unison, both.

When we get to Mum's, Two comes inside to tell Mum she's going to the hospice: 'I want to be with him.' She leaves. Three and I wait for Mum to ready herself, then, with Three behind the wheel, we arrange ourselves in Mum's car and take off for Bethlehem.

~

All the tubes, the plastic pouches and feeder lines, the life-support paraphernalia, was removed a day or two ago, so here he lies, peaceful, unencumbered by all that medical apparatus, his hair combed, his face shaved. A smoothed-out blanket neatly covers his body. His eyes are closed. Peaceful peacenik. The bedside lamp glows softly, as it has day and night for the past ten days – his dying days – here, in Bethlehem.

~

Sometimes, when I think about none of us being with him when he dies, I remember something Bernadette told me when she was trying to encourage Mum to send him to Bethlehem: there are times, she explained, when patients wait until their room – at home, in a hospital, wherever they are – is emptied of visitors, of family and friends, so they can die alone, in peace.

This information doesn't much assuage my anger with myself, or my interminable guilt, but it does make me wonder if what she said is so. If it is, then I marvel yet again at the capacities of the human brain. At the brain of the patient who, often unconscious, can still make such a determination, and at the brains of the scientists who ascertain that this is how it works.

~

He misses his one hundred and twenty by forty years, seven months and six days. Damn.

Dear Friends:
An email post-mortem

A quick note to let you know that Dad died at two this morning. He died peacefully and, as far as we could tell, was not in pain.

I am sad and weepy, but relieved, and proud and so glad to have been part of the process.

The funeral, an affair that's expected to be large, will be on Friday. The weather's forecast to be fine.

Apart from being exhausted down to my bone marrow (no sleep for 48 hours), I'm OK.

As to having been involved in the process of Dad's dying – well, I wouldn't have missed it for anything. In my life there have been few events as powerful.

I'll be in touch again soon.

Lots of love, Sandra

The Funeral, the Memorial and Going to Shul

What form will the funeral take? We know he wanted to be cremated, but what else? We agree there will be two events: the funeral for family, friends, a few close colleagues, and then, some time after that, a public memorial.

Sister Two doesn't want his coffin to be on display at the funeral.

'Oh, for goodness sake,' Mum snaps, snapping being a rare element of her relationship with Two, 'it's a funeral. We'll get them to drape something over the coffin if that makes you feel better.'

～

Sister Three makes the arrangements. In accordance with his wishes, his tape of Fauré's *Requiem* is given to the funeral parlour to play as people enter the chapel. When, well into my adulthood, I learn of his love of liturgical music, it comes as a surprise as I have no memory of hearing such music in our home during my childhood. Even more of a surprise – a shock, almost – is when, some years after he dies, Mum tells me during one of our sit and chat sessions in her car while parked out front of my apartment block, how much Dad loved listening to

Wynton Marsalis. 'He was a very big fan,' she says. Really? Jazz? Dad? Why did he never talk with me about that? Why don't I know until now? I wish I had known so we could have had conversations about jazz. We never did, and to this day I remain puzzled as to why.

What of the memorial? Sister Two wants it to be an intimate event, small.

'Not me,' I say. 'I want it to be bigger than *Ben Hur*.'

And so it becomes.

~

The Le Pines chapel at The Necropolis Springvale – these days more appealingly, more appropriately named Springvale Botanical Cemetery – is packed to the rafters. People file in to the strains of the Fauré.

Dad's pinewood coffin is draped in a drift of printed floral fabric, which could not be less appropriate.

Sister Three delivers a moving eulogy. Two stands by her side, a supportive presence. Three's eulogy is not without gentle criticism, but it is moving all the same. Or perhaps because. 'He was my father and I loved him,' she concludes.

Toby, the golden-haired grandson, takes the opportunity of delivering his eulogy to criticise his parents, Sister Two and her first husband, and to say how grateful he is that during fraught times in his childhood Sam was always there for him.

Tearfully, Ezra speaks of their near lifelong friendship and their comradely struggles for peace, both of which endured over decades. He does not mention that politically they choose different paths: while Dad continues to follow Moscow's authoritarian line, Ezra, along with other friends and the majority of Communist Party members, moves, after the Soviet invasion of Czechoslovakia, towards the less authoritarian, more modern – more democratic – Eurocommunism of Italy and France, and envisage a similar version for Australia.

～

An ABC News reader announces the official demise of the Soviet Union on a night I happen to be visiting my parents. Dad, who must surely have seen this collapse coming, is slumped in his rocker. Collapsed into himself, it could be said.

From this day forward, he goes into a serious decline. Depression is his daily grind. What must this mean to him? I wonder. His whole life, loyal. Against all criticism, loyal. Against all evidence, loyal.

I wonder if, during his life and sometimes after, his loyalty is such that what he says in public in defence of the Soviet Union and its eastern European allies, particularly the German Democratic Republic – East Germany – is the way a loyal devotee of any cause or person or religion would support the object of their dreams, their fantasies, their desires. Their projections. Are his public utterances what he really thinks? What he really feels? What he really knows? Does he genuinely believe there is no antisemitism in the Soviet Union? Does he genuinely believe, as he says before the political marriage between the Soviet Union and China ends in divorce and he is equally supportive of both (for a time at least), that there is, after the Chinese revolution, no longer any hunger in China? No prostitution? That the Chinese, under the guidance of the CCP, have eradicated all flies from the nation (as if that were a good thing)? Or does he know other truths and saves his criticisms for conversations with comrades, people he feels he can trust to make the criticisms with, in quiet places, unheard by detractors?

What does it mean to him that his whole life has been based around the notion of an idealised state and the form it takes in the workers' paradise, the Union of Soviet Socialist Republics, now that this notion has been swept away, that the oligarchs are stepping up and capitalism, the new broom, has swept in?

'Dad,' I say gently as I sit on a chair alongside his rocker, 'this must be terrible for you.' I take his hand.

He is unable to speak, but very slightly nods a couple of times. Is he going to cry? It seems so, but he doesn't.

'It must be …' I begin, nervous of his likely disapprobation; all the same, I push myself forward … 'like someone who believes in god most of their life, and then something happens to make them realise that god doesn't exist. All that wasted faith, wasted time and devotion.'

Just for a moment, his hand stiffens in mine. Then he relaxes his grip. He sighs.

'Yes,' he says, reluctant all the same, 'I suppose it is. It makes me wonder what my life has been about. Wasted.' Slowly, he shakes his head in a gesture of disbelief, of sorrow. Then, firmly, he says, 'I don't want to talk about this anymore, Sandy,' and lets go of my hand.

That is where it is left. We don't talk about this anymore. Understanding, yes, it's there, but nothing more said. His sadness, which lasts for the remainder of his life, makes me sad for him. Poor old coot. Poor Dad.

Later, I will wonder about his loyal devotion to his idealised Soviet Union and my loyal devotion to my idealised father, or at the very least to his ideas about the world: how it's run, how it should be. My loyal devotion to my idealised loyal Dad.

~

The remainder of the funeral is a blur. Eulogies over, people file out of the chapel and gather in the sunshine in groups of three, four, five. I remember many people, including me, lighting up cigarettes. I remember the funeral parlour offers to drive Mum and her daughters in one of their limousines to wherever we want to go, but we tell them we have Mum's car and will go together in that. Thank you very much. Or was that offer made when Mum died?

People drive off, along the roads through the graves in the cemetery's rose gardens, heading towards Caulfield. Mum has hired Tudor Hall, a function place whose destiny is to become an aged care facility. It is located in Kooyong Road, the road that has been the route to and from so much of what has happened in our lives these past several years. Mum permits the Tudor Hall staff to prepare and serve all the food and drink, albeit under her strict instruction.

For weeks to come, Mum says, 'I can't cry, you know.' She doesn't understand why. In fact, it will be two years before she rings me to say she has – 'finally' – shed tears over the loss of the husband with whom, for around sixty years, she has a loving if oft times ambivalent marriage.

~

South Melbourne Town Hall is hired for the public memorial. This venue is not a random choice: it is a symbolic gesture. It is here in 1959 that the inaugural public meeting of the Congress for International Cooperation and Disarmament is held, as are many subsequent public antiwar meetings.

Once again the space is packed. Some relatives – mostly immediate family, as well as his sister-in-law Valda, Mum's sister-in-law Mim and some of our cousins – have come. Peep is present. As well, activists, state and federal parliamentarians and friends; there are many mourners none of us know at all.

'G'day, Sandra,' says Tom Uren. 'Sorry about your dad. He was a good bloke.' Tom shakes my hand so firmly I think my knuckles are going to crack.

'Thanks, Tom.'

Mum is pleased to see Dad's cardiologist, Dr Jeff, who comes over to greet us. He and Dad become close over the years. Among the crowd are many peace activists, Labor Party and former Communist Party members, trade unionists (rank and file as well as past and current officials), acquaintances who hardly knew him but know of, participated in, the antiwar work he did over decades and respect him for that. There is handshaking, sad faces, condolences, remarks about what a great man he was, sympathies …

Having said I will deliver a speech, at the last minute I freeze. I am terrified, unable to move from my seat to the platform, a good 2 metres up from ground level, to address the crowd. Sister Two, who wanted to be the family member to speak, does not step up. With nothing prepared, and no thanks to me, she has missed the moment. She is furious with me.

~

Some time after the memorial service, I bump into former parliamentarian Clyde Holding and his wife, Judy, outside Readings in Acland Street. After a round of hellos, Clyde says, 'How's Sam?'

Clyde so shocks me that I am not alert enough, and so rush in: 'Clyde, you spoke at his memorial service only six months ago.'

'Did I?'

Judy has stepped back a couple of paces behind him. Gently, she shakes her head. Too late, I realise that Clyde must be in the early stages of dementia. Judy will phone later to tell me this is so.

～

What do the speakers say? How many were there? Why do I remember seven? Tribute givers who recall aspects of his life and their work with him who I do remember include Labor parliamentarians Tom Uren and Clyde Holding, and Save Our Sons founding member Jean McLean, who herself subsequently becomes a Labor state parliamentarian. The high-ceilinged hall resonates with their voices; each of them is well practised in addressing and holding a crowd. Was there afternoon tea? Most likely sandwiches, tea, coffee. Cakes probably, and biscuits. I cannot imagine Mum being in charge of any function where 'refreshments', that strange term, are not provided. So, yes, most likely there is afternoon tea.

～

Once again we pile into Mum's car, once again with Three at the wheel. We leave South Melbourne and head to Mum's house. Marching inside – really marching – I say to no one in particular, 'Give me a *fu*cking whiskey.' I steam towards the liquor tray, grab the decanter by the throat and look around to see who else wants one. As ever, only Sister Three does not.

I pour. *Splash, splash.* Drop two iceblocks into Mum's glass. *Plink, plink.* Soda into Sister Two's. *Swoooshh.*

Glasses. *Clink, clink, clink.*

'*L'chaim.*'

L'fucking chaim. To fucking life.

~

The Saturday after he dies, I attend shul at Temple Beth Israel. I hand in a slip of paper with his name written on it so he will be named along with others who have died this past week. Dr Andrew, his gastroenterologist, is also there. Dr Andrew is a regular at this synagogue. At first I don't see him, but as I walk past where he and his wife sit, he touches my arm. 'Sandra.' I smile, pleased to see him. 'I'm so sorry about your father,' he says.

'Thanks, Andrew.' After a short pause, through which he patiently waits, I continue. 'You know, even though it's been only four days, I miss him already.'

'Sandra,' he says, 'I'll tell you something. My mother died twenty years ago and there's not a day goes by that I don't think about her, not a week when I don't miss her.' He gives my arm a gentle squeeze.

'Thanks, Andrew,' I say, and move off to find myself a seat. Meeting him in the synagogue makes me smile.

~

Mum and I sit in her car outside my apartment building. We have been to a concert at Hamer Hall.

'Why wouldn't you be interested in …' She mentions the name of a widower roughly her age.

'Are you kidding?'

243

'Why not?'

Not for the first time my mother recommends this man as a potential partner for me, refusing to acknowledge how frequently I tell her I am not interested in having a partner, and if I were, it would surely not be this man. The conversation has always gone the same way.

'Too old, too square,' I reply. 'How many times do I have to tell you?'

'Well, who then? There has to be someone.'

'Oh, for god's sake, Mum. There doesn't have to be someone. I'm content with my life the way it is.'

'Who?' she insists.

I think for a moment.

'OK,' I concede, grinning, 'Dr Andrew.'

'Dr Andrew? Why him?'

'He'd be perfect for me. He's smart, has a sympathetic manner, he's Jewish, and he works such long hours that it's likely he'll hardly ever be at home.'

We laugh heartily.

Kiss, kiss.

'Good night, Mum.'

'Good night, Sandy.'

Burial

Although it's against Jewish religious law (and why would that bother him?), Dad wants to be cremated. He doesn't care what we do with his residue. With the residue of him.

Hmm.

We don't know what to do. The man at the funeral parlour says, in that professionally cloying voice, if we are unable to make up our minds, we may leave the ashes there for up to three months, after which time the parlour will get in touch with one of us to see how we are going with our decision. As I am the only sister living in Melbourne, and, to put not too fine a point on it, who cares what happens to his remains, and as Mum doesn't want to deal directly with this matter, I am designated.

Sister Two takes some of the ashes home with her, where, she later tells me, she incorporates him into one of her garden paths. So she can walk all over him? The rest remain at the parlour, awaiting our decision.

∼

The three months pass. The man from the funeral parlour rings. What would we like to do? I ring Mum.

'I don't know, Sandy. What do you think?'

'They'll let us leave him for another three months if we like.'

Mum doesn't want to do that.

In an inspired moment, I suggest we phone Port Phillip Council to ask if we can donate a rose – a Peace, of course – to the local botanic gardens and bury Dad there, beneath it. Mum likes the idea of his remains being laid to rest in St Kilda, where she has lived almost all of her life and where he lives for all but about ten or so of his seventy-nine years. It pleases her that he might be scattered in the gardens where he walked. 'Go on,' she says, 'do that. Arrange it.'

~

The switchboard operator at Port Phillip City Council puts me through to the gardening department. The woman at the other end of the line is taken aback. 'Oh,' she says, 'no one's ever asked for *that* before.' She has to ask someone if it's alright. She will get back to me within a week, she says.

Half an hour later, she calls back. She has taken our request to the mayor, who, it happens, knew Dad and admired him. Mum tells me that the mayor's father and Dad were Leftie friends years ago. Permission is granted for us to carry out our plan, but under no circumstances is there to be any visible evidence that anyone's ashes are buried in the gardens. 'We don't want the gardens looking like a cemetery,' the mayor cautions.

It is agreed that one of the gardeners will buy the Peace rose. When we gather, she will dig a hole in the rose garden, we will deposit some of the ashes in the hole and she will plant the rose on top of them. Of him. The remainder of the ashes will be scattered – unobtrusively – over the bed.

Next day I go to collect the ashes.

〜

The local Le Pines funeral parlour on Carlisle Street, near the corner of St Kilda Road, has long since been sold off and replaced by – what else? – an apartment block. But at the time I collect Dad's ashes, it is a tall, plain, cream brick building with white faux Doric columns. A circular driveway loops around the front of the building. In the middle of this loop is a small selection of standard roses, mostly pink. The roses stand in a patch of green lawn, though at the time Dad's body is taken in the hearse from here to the Springvale cemetery, the lawn is still parched brown from summer's heat. Cyprus pines, almost as tall as the building, line the east fence.

There are no funerals in progress when I arrive. There are a few cars in the driveway, but no one in sight. Inside, a uniformed woman – navy business jacket and matching straight skirt, white blouse, sensible black pumps – greets me with professional warmth, invites me to sit in the waiting room and goes off to find Dad's remains.

Ten minutes pass. Not another human is to be seen or heard. I become agitated; it feels too soon to be back here and the quiet is unsettling.

Another two or three minutes pass. Anxious, I step outside, stand under the portico, roll a cigarette and inhale deeply. A man also in a Le Pines uniform, walks hurriedly from the street around one side of the driveway, nods to me as he passes and goes inside.

For the customary ten minutes it takes me to smoke a cigarette I remain outside. Then I return to the foyer. Another fifteen or so minutes pass before the woman returns. In her hand she holds an elegant shopping bag: glossy royal blue with thick sky blue cotton rope handles. No logo, no text to be seen on the bag. Very discreet.

The woman places the bag on a bench. I peer into it. Inside is a squat plastic tub, more like a bottle, in blues matching the bag: royal blue for the tub, sky blue for the lid. When the Le Pines woman passes me the bag, I am surprised by how heavy it is, even considering the quantity Sister Two took with her, although I have no idea how much that might be.

What do I feel, seeing this plastic tub, knowing that what's inside it are the remains of my father's corporeal self? Not much, I have to say: not sad, not disturbed, not afraid. Perhaps a bit amused. Odd? Possibly. Numb? Possibly.

~

What paperwork there is that requires my signature is soon despatched. I thank the woman and leave. The bag is so sophisticated, its colours so glamorous. Later, I tell Mum that I felt as if I'd just come from a shopping jaunt at Bergdorf Goodman or Barney's ('Where?' she says), two upmarket New York emporia where, in all my many stays in New York, I never once shopped due to their maximalist prices and my minimalist budget, though I did once go to Barney's to have a look around.

Back on Carlisle Street, I see in the distance that my tram, an old rattler, is heading my way. The tram and I arrive at the stop at the same time. I board, settle into a seat, put my package on the floor by my feet and look around.

On board is the usual mixture of number 16 passengers: the hip, the benighted, the poor, the chic, Russian and Israeli immigrants, mums with kids, teenagers wagging school, locals. Tourists, of course; backpackers and older travellers of apparently greater means.

It is a struggle to keep from giggling. Among this motley crew, only I know that there are no fancy shoes or clothes in the gorgeous bag at my feet – just flesh burnt to ash and chips of bone. My dad is in there. My desire to giggle dissipates as tears begin to trickle down my cheeks. I wipe them away with my fingers.

At last the tram arrives at Luna Park, where I alight and walk across O'Donnell Gardens to Spenser Street, down the street to my apartment.

Ten minutes after I get inside and set him down on the floor, the phone rings.

'Have you got him?' Mum says.

'I have,' I tell her. She is sniffling. 'But I'm not sure where to put him.'

'Oh god,' she gasps, 'don't leave him where anyone can carry him off.'

'It's alright, Mum,' I say with a smile, 'he'll be in the apartment, with me. He's alright.'

'Remember to lock the door,' she says.

Ghosts, spirits, the likes of these don't bother me, though I have to admit that the evening does feel a bit ghoulish having Dad, neatly placed, resting in a plastic bottle in the tiny hallway at my front door.

Before I retire for the night, I tell him that tomorrow morning I am taking him to the St Kilda Botanical Gardens, where we will be met by Mum, two of his adult grandchildren (one of my children,

Sister Three's son), his sister-in-law and a family friend. After that, I bid him goodnight and take myself to bed.

~

The next morning, bag in tow, I walk across Peanut Farm to Blessington Street and up the street to the gardens. It is a lovely morning: sunny, warm, a light sea breeze. Again, there is that same feeling I have on the tram, the feeling that I have a delightful secret.

As I enter the garden gates, I hasten my step. When I come around a bend in the path, I can see Mum and others gathered by the gazebo in front of the rose garden. Even from this distance, it is clear Mum is agitated.

'Where have you been?'

'It's OK, Mum. I'm here now.' There is no point in reminding her that I have arrived with ten minutes to spare. 'Where is the gardener?' I ask.

No one in our little party seems to know, which causes more consternation, but only a few minutes later, at the appointed time, we see her striding along the path, coming towards us. She is carrying a bare-rooted rose bush and a shovel.

She greets us with nods and a hello, with a mixture of kindness and curiosity. Who are these people the mayor has granted permission to conduct this burial? We reply with our own nods and hellos. Then, the gardener holds up the rose. At once, I see that the label displays a deep red bloom, not the soft, pink-tinged lemony yellow of a Peace.

'No, no, not that,' I wail. 'Not that red one.' I start to cry. 'I asked for a Peace. It has a particular significance for us. We wanted a Peace.'

They don't have one, the gardener explains. This one, she says, is a lovely rose with a beautiful scent. 'No, no, no.'

'Alright. What if we go to the shed to see if we can find one there?'

Still holding onto the blue bag (why don't I leave it with Mum? why am I making such a fuss?), I scurry off after the gardener, down the path to the work shed, leaving my mother and our family members bemused, probably annoyed, probably agitated, standing in a group alongside the gazebo.

There is no Peace rose in the potting shed. There has not been a Peace in the potting shed for some time. Because it is clear how upset I am, the gardener says that if I like she can order in a Peace, but if I agree to that, it means coming back to bury and scatter Dad's ashes in a couple more weeks when the rose arrives.

Deflated, I tell her that I don't want to have to do this again, that Mum certainly would not want to and most likely nor would the other family members, so we return, she and I, more slowly this time, along the path to where my family is waiting.

⁓

Council, probably the gardening division, determines that Dad is to be buried in the rose garden we are standing by, a large bed full of the same variety of dark red rose the gardener brings us. Resigned, everyone agrees that we accept this one. In the end, we agree it is enough that he is going to be buried there, in that bed in the gardens.

The gardener digs a suitably sized hole. We agree to dispose of Dad's ashes by everyone taking a turn: pass the bottle, shake some ashes into the hole, and then pass the bottle on to the next.

Calm settles on me.

~

My grandson, then five, and I are walking towards the horizon along Brookes Jetty, opposite Edgewater Towers, the apartment block on Marine Parade where I live. Coming towards us are about twenty people walking in single file (the jetty is too narrow to hold more than a single file each way). They are not formally dressed, no suits, no ties, no dressy frocks. They look sombre. The person in the front of the line is carrying a large lidded container.

'What are you doing?' my grandson asks the line leader.

'Our loved one died,' he replies. 'We've been scattering their ashes.'

Which leads my grandson to have a conversation with me about people dying, what dying means and why people who die become ashes. Some time later he will ask me if I am going to die too and I will break his heart.

~

We pour in as much residue as the hole has capacity to contain while still leaving space for the rose. Mum takes charge of the tub, shakes out what little remains inside it and sprinkles it over the topsoil. Within two minutes, the bottle is empty.

What to do with the tub and the bag? The gardener sees Mum's quandary. 'Would you like me to dispose of that for you?' she offers.

Gratefully, Mum hands her the bag with the now empty plastic bottle inside it and thanks her. The gardener retrieves her shovel and, carrying it in one hand, the blue items in her other, bids us good day and leaves.

I watch as she recedes along the path towards the potting shed.

'Come on,' Mum says as she dusts off her hands. 'Let's go home and have a cup of tea.'

~

Six months later, on 31 December, two events occur, each by means of a phone call.

The first comes at around eleven o'clock. It's Cousin Annie.

'Sandy, I always used to ring your Dad on his birthday and have a chat,' she says. 'I decided to keep up the tradition by ringing you.'

And so it has been for these past many years. Sometimes we talk about Dad for a while, remember him for better or worse; sometimes we don't talk about him at all. On the occasions he is part of our conversation, we move on after a while to more general matters. Cousin Annie warms my heart.

The second phone call is from Mum, who phones on the morning of New Year's Eve, seven months after he dies, to ask if I would like to accompany her to the gardens to visit Dad. 'It's his birthday today you know.' As if I would forget. 'I thought I'd go and sit in that gazebo, keep him company for a while.'

She offers to pick me up on the way. Even though I live no more than twelve minutes' walk from the gardens, even though her driving makes me nervous – especially when she passes parked cars with barely a hair's breadth between them and her, or when she stops in the middle of a road to let an elderly person cross despite there being no lights, no crossing – I accept her offer.

~

We arrive at the gardens without incident, park in Tennyson Street and walk along the neat path that runs through the equally neat lawn to the gazebo, where we sit facing the rose garden.

For about half an hour, we sit quietly together. Occasionally, Mum brings forth a memory. Mostly we don't speak; we just sit, contemplating. Then, 'Ready?' Mum says.

'Whenever you are,' I reply.

Slowly, we stand up from the gazebo bench. I walk her through the gardens back to her car, and then, after I tell her I'll walk back, I take the long way home, along Dickens Street.

∽

Cousin Annie continues to call every year on new year's eve. I continue to light a *yahrtzeit* candle on the anniversary of his death. Mum and I add Dad's birthday to the date of my parents' wedding anniversary to go to the gazebo. There, on each occasion, we spend half an hour to an hour, quiet, pensive, most often just sitting, occasionally talking. Sometimes we read. Sometimes we hold hands, keeping gentle company in a rose garden wherein lies a scattering of ashes and bone chips that no one but us, a few family members and the gardener know are there.

∽

Nine years later, Mum dies. Even though I continue to live that short walk from the gardens, I never visit Dad again.

Letter to Sister Two, Post Facto

Dear Two

I know what you mean about those last days (is it alright to talk about them?). Among my abiding images – they aren't all bad, but these are the two worst – (1) walking into Dad's last room at Cabrini and seeing him so dishevelled, with only half his pyjama jacket on, only one button done up and most of his torso uncovered, and his tooth out, and (2) the shock of the prison-like single room after the sunny multiple-bed room he was first in at Bethlehem. I berate myself constantly for not having railed more at the Cabrini people about him being so uncared for because of my fear that, having said something once and asked them to dress him properly, if I persisted they would treat him worse … I couldn't help feeling contempt for the whole place.

I don't know if you want to talk about this at all, and I know you said you try to keep it in the background, so I'll desist, but if you ever do …

What a cruel fate to be a person such as Mum is, unable to accept help from people. The last thing she said this morning when I left to go home was 'No thanks, dear, I have to be able to do all this for myself.' It makes me angry and sad and frustrated to the nth degree. You probably know that Ess offered to come to stay a few nights, Zee offered to come with the baby and stay on Thursday or Friday and again later, but she turned them all down. I don't think she even realises that it might be a nice thing for her granddaughters to do. She kept insisting that I go home too, but even though I hadn't planned to stay, I could see that she was whacked and that really she did want me to. When I said I was staying, the relief on her face and in her voice was so obvious. Sheez. In its own way, this lack of grace is harder to deal with than actually being there.

She overdid it wildly yesterday, having only a little lie down for about half an hour in the mid arvo (I'm not even sure if that's the truth; she may not have had any lie down at all). By the time she went to bed at nine, she looked grey and was exhausted.

As for me, I'm feeling relieved as well as excited that I'm going away for a few weeks. Did I tell you that I'm staying … yes, I did … Vancouver Island on my way to New York? God, the way I feel right now, I wish my friend's son wasn't coming to visit and thus kicking me out of my – his – bed so I could spend an extra week in the wilds of the Pacific Northwest. I do love it up there. But one (I) can be quiet in NY as well as racing around; I'm sure there'll be a bit of both. I went to buy The New Yorker to see what's on in my zones of interest. I just had a quick look through it and that was enough to pump me up a few notches.

Last week I went to listen to what I thought was going to be jazz, but it turned out to be … well, the only way I can think of to describe it is heavy Latin. It started off OK and I liked the first three or four numbers, but then it got heavier and heavier and louder and louder. Too much for this ol' chook. When we arrived at The Continental I was aware of all the blokes there. Later, Andra said that the drummer and bass player are hot items among drummers and bass players and that the former is giving a 4 day drum clinic after the Wangaratta Jazz Fest, hence all the blokes at the gig.

Do you like The Continental? I love it as a place for music and have always felt it was one of those places a woman of any age can go alone and feel comfortable. Being there (the first time out listening to music in ages) made me feel I was back in my life again.

I thought I was going to be working right up to departure moment, but a wicked author is taking much longer than she should to get her corrections done, so when I've finished what I'm doing now, which will be Monday a.m., I'll be able to get myself in order at my leisure, relaxed knowing that dosh will be coming in. Oh what a feeling!

That said, I'd best be off and get cracking with this job, or someone will call me a wicked editor.

Perusing the Files

Time has come to read the ASIO files. His, mine. In a form reply to my application, the National Archives of Australia informs me it takes up to ninety days for the files to be ready.

I wait.

And wait.

Four months pass. I phone. 'How much longer before the files are available?'

'We'll let you know.'

Do I imagine it, or is his tone terse?

Around twelve months from the time I apply, a letter from the NAA arrives: the files are ready.

Manning Clark House, as well as being a venue for cultural and political events, rents rooms to out of town writers and researchers. After arranging flights to and from Canberra, I book myself in for several nights.

Over the next few years, I take up residence at Manning Clark House three times. It is a joy to be there.

~

Set in lovely grounds – bright green lawns, rhododendron bushes, camellias, roses, nasturtiums, cornflowers, herb and vegetable gardens – Manning Clark House, designed by Robin Boyd, is imposing yet comfortable. Its walls whisper histories of its original residents, historian and academic Manning Clark, his linguist wife Dymphna (why isn't it called Manning and Dymphna Clark House?) and their six children, as well as all the people who visited them there.

One room, once a bedroom, serves now as an office where the House director and manager work. The other bedrooms are for the likes of me: writers who create time for themselves away from their daily lives to write in uninterrupted peace. Other guests carry out and read the research that will inform their writing.

As it happens, on this first occasion I am the only resident.

My friend Sal picks me up at the airport; later we go out for dinner. Soon after she drops me off at the House, I fall into bed and have a deep and satisfying sleep.

Each morning Sal and I go into Kingston for coffee and croissants and the continuation of the conversation we've been having for the past twenty years. An hour later she deposits me at the NAA.

~

On the long tables in the reading room of the National Archives sit a few short, semiclear plastic boxes that contain batches of freshly sharpened wood pencils for researchers to use. No pens allowed. The tables, a blondish semiglossed timber, are clear of anything else. Compared to my own desk, it is thrilling to sit at, to work at, tables like these because me, I'm a spreader; on my desk, barely a square inch is left uncovered. Not that a pristine desk is my objective; it's not.

Messy desk is just how I am, who I am. More than once, when staying at a friend's house, the occasion's home owner pulls me into line for spreading myself into more of their space than they would like me to have, than what's on offer. They tell me I'm taking it over.

An uncluttered workspace is more of a fantasy in which I imagine an almost empty desk with nothing on it but my computer and keyboard. The desk would stand in a white painted room with only a half a dozen of my favourite paintings and photographs on the walls – or, if I were to be really daring, no hangings at all – and a vase stand on which a decorative glass vase is filled with a bunch of flowers or leaves, bay laurel for example, fresh each week. But in my heart I know this sparse workroom will forever remain a fantasy, because really, I am just not a cleared desk, sparse workroom kind of woman.

Which makes it a delight to arrive each morning into a reasonable facsimile of my fantasy space. Others with similar purpose – I presume – share this large room. Our studious presence creates a calming atmosphere; it exudes a sense of quiet industrious endeavour. Heads down, we go about our business as we study files, write in notebooks, key information into laptops.

On day one, after obtaining the files – there are twenty of them, each containing two hundred pages – I settle into a chair, remove a pencil from its box and sit back, staring at the pile of folders.

Each bundle of two hundred A4 pages is secured in a buff-coloured manila folder. On the front of each folder is an A4 sheet, a form of some kind or another, of which I take little notice; what's typed there looks to be catalogue numbers.

A sense of excited anticipation and nervousness begins to build. What will I find here? Will there be information about his life that I don't already know? Will there be material that will shock me?

Will I read things that I will wish I had never seen? Information that will please or mortify me?

I open file one. Begin.

⌒

Four elements of the pages surprise me. The first is that his year of birth is given as 1917. We have always known it to be 1919. What does this mean? An ASIO error (it too makes mistakes)? Something else? Some while after sighting this date, a glimmer of a memory flickers on. Do I remember correctly that he tells me he falsified his age upwards by two years so he could join up? That can't be it because when I do the sums, it's obvious that, were he born in 1917, he would be twenty-four or five in 1941, the year he joins the airforce – once he was convinced the war was against Hitler's Germany, not against the Soviet Union. Where does this memory come from?

The second is that although I anticipate seeing thick black redaction lines in these ASIO files, unlike the Special Branch files, almost no black lines are evident, with the exception of one page. It is a report of a Coburg Communist Party branch meeting. The blacked-out material is a list of meeting attendees. Why bother? If one of the comrades on the list is the rat, who would know which person that might be? Apart from the rat, of course. Why not just leave all the names there for a researcher to see? Besides, of the ten or so names that are hidden, I know I can name at least half of them. The remaining redactions – strikethrough or whiteout marks – are, for the most part, the names of operatives.

The third curious element is the paucity of information. As I read through these files, I realise after a day or so that they are much depleted, that whatever it is I am hoping, even expecting, to find in them isn't here. What that is I would be hard-pressed to say, but to my great disappointment, it isn't here.

What I find is copies of agendas and meeting minutes, mostly of the Vietnam Moratorium Campaign; an occasional agenda from a Communist Party branch meeting; details of phone calls to the house and to the Peace Council office. There are lists of numberplates of the cars of people attending meetings, an occasional reference to an overseas trip Dad takes and, not infrequently, bits and pieces of incorrect information.

The number of errors is the fourth thing that surprises me: people's names, misspellings, places, connections between this person and that. Some time into my research I take delight in using an NAA pencil to correct some of the errors, corrections I pencil into the margin. What difference can it make?

⁓

Most significant of these points is the paucity of information, of details. This keeps me wondering for a long time to come; indeed, until my third examination of the files, and again, much later.

All the pages appear to be photocopies of original documents: no beverage stains on the paper, no yellowing from cigarette smoke or age, no rumpling or creases or folds. Pristine A4 pages. All the pages recount meetings attended, public meetings addressed or meetings with individuals, Communist Party officials, peace movement activists, peace movement donors and the comings and goings of people to our house. None of the pages I read have anything to say about his travels to the Soviet Union to attend World Peace Council meetings or his travels to other parts of Europe, usually for political reasons, combined with tourism. Wouldn't that be of some significance? The only entry I find about his travels is when he meets a couple on a return to Australia, on a KLM – Royal Dutch Airlines – flight. Are they the ones who put him in to ASIO? Is that why they are there? To let a reader, anyone in his family, for example, know that the ubiquitous 'they' were keeping an eye on him?

Nothing here about his philandering. Does a person of interest's affairs – casual or more serious, such as the one with the French journalist or the one with Peep – count adequately to be included in ASIO or Special Branch files? Seems not. Or perhaps this information, as well as the travel information, is part of what's been redacted. Frustration makes me twitchy.

While there are plenty of reports of phone calls to and from the Goldbloom household, to and from the CICD office, it is baffling to find very, very few transcripts of those calls, though there are transcripts of calls between other people about Dad, about us.

I cast a glance over mostly uninteresting material about who he marries (know that), who his children are (know that) and which meetings he attended this week or that (know plenty of that). There are notes about who his daughters marry (sure as hell know that), an occasional page about one or another Party official talking about him with another Party member, but nothing that excites my interest. From time to time, I doze off over the file that's opened in front of me. Am I missing things? Misreading? Can the collection really be this dull? Can the collection be so lacking in information? Seems so.

Just what is it I'm hoping to find? All I can say is I'm looking.

~

On my first day in the archives, having set to work at around 9.30, I realise it is well after one and I have not had – nor wanted – a cigarette. Almost four hours. A record. Never mind that the information is frustratingly scant; I have been engrossed enough to not even think about going out for a smoke. Right now I wouldn't mind a smoke, but more still, some food. Someone points me in the direction of a cafe and I head off on a stroll beneath fluttering trees, past rose beds to the cafe.

As comfortable as the NAA room is, after almost four hours of nose to the pages it is a pleasure to be outdoors in the sunshine. I order a sandwich and a coffee and find myself a table on the cafe's deck. Just as I'm tapping a cigarette out of its packet, a passing waiter gives me a rueful smile, raises his eyebrows and wags a *no no no* finger at me. 'Sorry, no smoking allowed in Canberra cafes,' he says.

Each day after that I buy my lunch – a baguette and a coffee – from the cart in the NAA foyer or bring takeaway from a local cafe. I sit on a nearby bench to eat, drink my coffee and smoke a cigarette or two. A passing parade of people I presume to be public servants – researchers, tourists perhaps – going about their day piques my curiosity. Who are they? What are they doing? Where are they going? While I sit, rose gardens behind me, a grassy patch in front with a view to the street through the trees, I ponder the uninformative pages.

～

My own files – four in all, also two hundred pages each – await me where I leave them, alongside Dad's, when I go out for lunch.

They contain the same disquieting lack of detail. A note about the enthusiasm with which I embrace feminism, who I marry, who my children are ... Do I find anything about moving to Canada the day after I marry? Not that I can see. Anything about Jack designing the moratorium badge, its stylised peace dove and several of its posters? Not a word. Anything about me working with Dad's friend and other antiwar activists in the Toronto peace movement helping American refusers and draft resisters who, seeking refuge, come across the border, where they are granted safe haven? About my task to help them find somewhere to stay? Nothing. About my peace movement activism from my mid teens to the date of the files? The concerts I organised to raise money, the screening of peace- or antiwar-themed films? *Gornisht. Niente. Nada.* My full-time activism in the Vietnam Moratorium Campaigns, recasting former Victorian Peace Committee groups in the suburbs and regional towns as local moratorium groups, helping local people create new suburban and regional moratorium groups and leaflet suburban shopping streets? Not a bloody word.

Fewer than a dozen photos are to be found in all these files. I ask the appropriate person to please photocopy them for me, but really, they are useless. For a time they sit in a folder in my file cabinet, until, after one last look some weeks after my return to Melbourne, I throw them away.

$\sim$

And so it goes. I work my way through the files in the hope of finding something that will illuminate, anything that will expand my knowledge, tell me something – significant or otherwise – I don't already know. Hope dashed.

Resolute, I continue to show up at the archives, return late each afternoon to Manning Clark House, have coffee with Sal each morning and try again. Three times I come to Canberra, for a fewer or a greater number of days.

On my returns to Melbourne, Sisters Two and Three enquire about what I find. There is little to tell them.

What is it I hope to find? Do I want to encounter a man even more heroic than the one I conjure up, who looms so large in my consciousness, in my unconscious? Do I want to find an arch villain, an agent of influence, a Soviet spy? Heaven forbid, an ASIO spy?

Such is the nature of unanswered – unanswerable – questions, of the fantasies they provoke. Wild, unabated, they make a run on one's attention, on *my* attention. Were villainy his mantle, would it make him even more of a hero to me, or repugnant? If I can't say, and I can't, then who can?

～

I phone Mavis Robertson, former joint national secretary of the Communist Party of Australia and antiwar activist. Mavis and Dad were on antiwar committees together. No love is lost between them.

'I'd like to talk to you about Dad.'

'Sure.' Her voice becomes unpleasant. 'There's quite a bit I can tell you about your father,' she says.

My feet turn cold; I become nervous. Two weeks later, a day or two before our arranged meeting, I phone to postpone the meeting. 'Not ready,' I say. 'It's too soon.' Do I hear her smirk or do I imagine it because of my lack of courage?

Two months later, I grit my teeth and try again.

I go to her ground-floor apartment in a renovated 1950s building. Her apartment is light, sunny. Noise from the busy east–west road is muffled by trees in her garden. Mavis is happy to see me. 'I'm glad you came,' she says as she ushers me into the lounge room. Looking around, I see that she too has been a tschatschkes collector. The apartment's surfaces and walls are covered with them. 'I don't know if I can be much use to you. I didn't really know your father very well, and I didn't have very much to do with him.' She smiles at me.

I want to cry out 'Liar' but I don't; she intimidates me and, with her response of two months earlier still resounding in my head, I am fearful of what she might say.

We have lunch, we natter – Mavis mostly talks about herself and her life, which is interesting enough, but nothing about Dad. Throughout the three hours we spend together, I do not press her.

When I recount this tale of frustration to a friend, a writer, the friend says, 'Did you take notes?'

'No,' I say.

'Did you sit at the tram stop and write it all down?'

I tell my friend that it didn't occur to me to do so because Mavis didn't have anything to tell me about Dad. For my troubles, I have my head blasted off.

Opportunity lost.

～

It is not until my third and final visit to the NAA that I come to understand what is going on, in the files, at least, if not in his life.

～

Time spent reading the files becomes shorter. With each visit my frustration grows; there seems to be little point. Still, I enjoy seeing Sal and hanging out with her on several evenings as well as in the mornings, and going together to galleries, walking in the park. I enjoy working in the NAA room, enjoy finding the sharpened pencils in their containers each morning, enjoy opening up another file, take great pleasure in walking around the area at lunchtime or just sitting on a bench, watching the passing parade. Enjoy, albeit fading, the hope, the expectation that comes with every file opening. Perhaps most of all, I enjoy the sense of quiet purpose that I and others have about us as we work. Is working in a university library like this? More than once it crosses my mind that it must be, and I smile.

~

One morning, sitting at the table, the stack of files unopened, I stare unseeing at an A4 page stapled to the cover of the manila folder as I ponder what's next. At first, in a kind of haze, all I see is the paper, the ink, undifferentiated words, ruled columns. After a few minutes, a gleam of light bounces off a staple and draws my eyes to focus on the page. For the first time in all the days of all the visits I have spent here, I read what is written across the top of the A4 sheet. Excited, astonished, I flip through the files: his, mine. *Next next next next.* Each says the same thing. At last, here it is. All my wondering, my puzzlement, explained.

Across the top of each cover sheet is typed an alphanumeric code, followed by the same words that explain why the files are so depleted. The codes are not some form of filing system, some NAA version of the Dewey decimal; no, they are, at least I presume when I first acknowledge them, citations from the *Crimes Act*. Redacted in the interests of national security, to paraphrase. Disappointing, but at least it's something of an explanation. It's something to go on.

~

Years later, while I am still writing this book, in a rush of curiosity I look up the NAA website for entries about Dad. After keying in his name, a landscape page comes up, Excel or somesuch; it contains a list of his files in numerical order. One column is headed 'Item Title', below which are listings of his name, a file volume number and a live link: 'Access status: Open with exception.' Once opened, a complete list of the codes governing the redactions is revealed. Information is provided – the full citation of each listed section of the Act – that explains why the redaction, why the absences, why the dreariness of the files.

While all this time I have presumed the redactions to be the due to ASIO's interpretation of the *Crimes Act*, I learn they refer to sections of the *Archives Act*. Does this mean the NAA, not the security organisations, decides what can be read? I write to the NAA to see if I have this right.

In the meantime, I read the relevant sections of the Act. They are these: '33(1)(a) – would damage Australia's security, defence or international relations', '33(1)(d) – would be a breach of confidence', '33(1)(e)(ii) – would, or could reasonably be expected to, disclose the existence or identity of a confidential source of information, including a person providing confidential information to the National Crime Authority or the Australian Federal Police or a witness under the *Witness Protection Act* 1994' and, finally, '33(1)(g) – would unreasonably disclose information about the personal affairs of a person'. Similar notations are listed on my files.

Yes, I do have it right. National Archives has a declassification section staffed by access examiners who make the decisions about what information in a file is permitted to be released so it can be read. A researcher may apply to have redacted material released. When I ask for the application form at the desk, the man in attendance says, 'I wouldn't bother if I were you.'

'Why not?'

He won't answer, but as things turn out, he is correct.

I submit the form. I wait. In time, a reply comes back via email to say, in effect, that after reviewing my request, no further information from the files will be forthcoming.

～

Once again Sister Two and I are in truce mode. Round number who knows what? That's how it is with us.

She calls to ask if it's alright with me if she reads the files.

I know what's coming, which puts me in a temper. 'You don't need my permission,' I snap. 'They are in the public domain.'

We hang up.

She goes to Canberra and reads his files. Does she read mine as well? I'm too angry to ask.

Some time later, we are both guests at the same event. Two describes some of what she reads in the files.

'That wasn't there,' I exclaim.

'It was,' she replies.

'Not when I looked.'

Sister Two mentions several other pages of material she sees in our father's files that I do not.

'Are you making this up?' My question is foolish, childish, and in my bones I know she isn't.

While we are talking, Sister Two opens her phone and begins to scroll. 'Here,' she says, 'look.' At the NAA she took photos of pages that interested her. What she shows me is material I do not recall seeing, not one line of it.

What on earth is going on? Why does she see files that aren't as redacted as the files I see? Might it be because when she applies for the files, the NAA does not know she is a Goldbloom? When I search her on the NAA site by her maiden name, she is not there. She is infrequently mentioned in Dad's or my files, at least on the pages I read, and most of what I read about her is who she marries. Is it my memory – have I forgotten some of what I saw? Are some of the pages Sister Two sees ones I fell asleep over?

There will never be any answers to these questions, I have come to realise, not for me at least. Sister Two's research comes up different to mine and neither of us will ever know the why of that either. But now, a long time after Dad is dead, a long time after I research his and my files at the NAA, what the redactions might have revealed no longer feels pressing. Were I to learn what the deleted information is, would it make any difference to me now? If I don't – won't ever – know what's there, how can I tell if it would upset me if I did know?

Today, more immediate concerns occupy my mind. The urgency has gone from the need to search for the finer points. Inadequate information, unfilled gaps: these no longer frustrate me. They no longer arouse my curiosity. The greater urgency is to complete this book. Whatever my memories – good, bad – they suffice. Indeed, they do better than suffice: today I am content with them.

⁓

Feeling claustrophobic, in need of some respite from my life, I fly to Canberra to I stay with Sal for a few days. We go to the National Gallery to see the exhibition of costumes from Sergei Diaghilev's Ballets Russes.

It is a beautiful collection, with many eye-catching pieces. We linger. We come to a piece that most draws my attention. It is a white-hooded coat with thick black arrowheads, vertebrae-like down the middle of its back (only the back is visible). Upturned isosceles triangles on the sleeves and shoulders follow the line of the spine. Later, I will learn that the coat's fabric is white felt and the appliquéd arrowheads and triangles are navy velvet, though they appear to me to be black. Because I know little about the Ballets Russes, *and even less about who designed the costumes, I am surprised to learn that this costume is designed by Henri Matisse.*

Will there be postcards of some of these costumes? I hope there are.

Sal and I continue on our way for some time, looking, admiring, exchanging opinions in soft voices.

In the foyer I see there is a selection of postcards depicting some of the costumes in the exhibition. My friend patiently waits while I make a beeline for the Matisse, fossick in my purse for some money, then go to the counter to pay for my cards – I buy three – and off we go.

Only when we get back to Sal's apartment does it occur to me to look at the back of the card to see if the coat has a name.

It does, of course: Costume for a Mourner.

Coda

On and off these past few days I've been weepy. Today in particular I am very weepy. Almost anything sets me off because today, 25 May 2023, is significant for me on two counts.

First, it happens to be Dad's *yahrtzeit*, the anniversary of his death, and second, it is the day I will hand over the completed manuscript of this book to my publisher.

~

To memorialise him and in keeping with Jewish tradition, I light the twenty-four-hour *yahrtzeit* candle. The candle flickers away on the bench as I write.

The coincidence of this timing puts me in mind of Peep's death, which occurs on my birthday.

Regarding the book, I know what's coming. The deflation that follows – for me, at least – the completion of a book, even of a story. There is such joy in sitting at the desk, clacking away on the keyboard, thinking, writing, wondering where in hell this or that idea sprang from, enjoying the surprise of a memory dredged up that, once it reveals itself, I realise I think of as long lost.

In the next few hours, this book will be completed, ready for editing. It is a manuscript that has, I like to say, taken longer to gestate than an elephant. Multiple gestations.

~

Twenty-three years have passed since Dad died, and I miss him still. Not all the time, but often. When some political event occurs – not least in the Middle East – I want to get on the phone so we can have a conversation. 'What do you think about this? … About that?' In his last years, it is not uncommon for me to disagree with him, often to his chagrin.

I miss our conversations, though our politics diverge enough during his life that we sometimes bicker – on interpretations, ways forward, the significance of environmentalism and feminism and racism and their place in the political spectrum. It was his belief that if world peace, along with nuclear and conventional weaponry disarmament, was not first achieved, there would be no women and girls left to fight for, no planet left to rescue, no racism to fight against. To me the issues are inseparable and immediate.

I miss the chyacking and the pleasure of pleasing him, especially with my cooking, as well as with birthday and spontaneous non-birthday presents. I miss being able to seek his advice. I miss seeing his pleasure when I remark on his latest haircut.

'Had a haircut, Dad?' Never miss a beat, me.

'Oh, you noticed,' he says, coquettish after each of the several times a year he visits the barber.

I miss showing off my achievements and his admiration of them.

~

The frustrations of secrets kept, of being able only to surmise, of the ongoing wondering, all these too diminish. In diminishing, they clear the air. Instead of so much wondering and anger, there is more room now for love and forgiveness.

Today, I like to think that, at least in my mind's eye, Dad is no longer the romanticised father, the idealised political mentor, though even if some of the sheen has been dulled, there remains some idealisation all the same. I still bristle when I hear people criticise him. I continue to hope I am something of the daughter he would like me to have been.

~

Twenty-oh-four or five. On the steps of the State Library. A rally is being held by Jews for a Just Peace, of which I am a founding and executive member. I address the crowd.

Some time later, as the crowd begins to disperse, several people, including some of Dad's contemporaries, come over to congratulate me. One participant, a man who knew Dad and has known me since I was a child, says, 'Sandra, your father would have been proud of you today.'

Without a second's hesitation, I reply: 'He was always proud of me.'

~

A loving if fallible parent, Dad was proud of me just as I was of him, as he was of his other two daughters and all of our achievements.

Really, though, when all is said and done, what matters most to me is that I loved him. And that he loved me.

275

Sandra Goldbloom Zurbo is the author of the novel *The Book of Rachel* (1998), which was also translated into German. Several of her short stories and poems have been published in literary magazines, including *Griffith Review* and *Westerly*. In 1982 Sandra established Dead Set, the first desktop publishing company to work specifically with book and journal publishers. For the past forty years, she has worked as a non-fiction editor and proofreader for leading academic and trade publishers. Born and raised in the Melbourne suburb of St Kilda, she now lives, gardens and writes in Castlemaine, in central Victoria.

Printed in the USA
CPSIA information can be obtained
at www.ICGtesting.com
JSHW080848300923
49443JS00004B/70